From Mourning to Morning

Discovering the Healing Power of
God's Love To Take You From Grief to Glory

by
Harry and Cheryl Salem

Harrison House
Tulsa, Oklahoma

From Mourning to Morning—Discovering the Healing Power of God's Love To Take You From Grief to Glory
ISBN 1-57794-377-5
Copyright © 2001 by Salem Family Ministries
P.O. Box 701287
Tulsa, OK 74170

Published by Harrison House
P. O. Box 35035
Tulsa, Oklahoma 74153

Dedication

Dear Gabrielle,

I told you when this horrible thing was all over that you would have your very own book. Well, here it is. Its ending is not exactly the one I had in mind, but nonetheless, to God be the glory. Your picture is on the cover, more wonderful photos of you are throughout, and your artwork is on the back cover. Even though it's only a glimpse of who you are, I believe God will use it to bless and restore those who read it. You are still changing lives, as you always have since the day you were born.

As I told you the day you left and went to heaven, when the Rapture comes, wait for me in the air—I'll be right behind you.

I love you,
Mama

Table of Contents

Acknowledgments

To the countless hundreds of thousands worldwide who prayed for our precious daughter, Gabrielle, we want you to know it was not in vain. Only when you get to heaven will you know how your prayers were answered. (Gabrielle is not only in our past, but is also in our future!)

To the multitudes of people who held up our arms through the battle and beyond, doing extraordinary things for Gabrielle and for our family, we want to say we love you from the bottom of our hearts. Your rewards are recorded in heaven.

To Gabrielle's earthly escorts on the day of her home-going celebration, we extend our thanks for bearing her up in your arms and in your hearts: Rev. Jess Gibson, Rev. Rocky Bezet, Rev. Ron Clark, Gary Gibson, Dr. Mike Ritze and Stan Tacker.

To the anointed men of God who shared God's Word and wisdom at Gabrielle's home-going celebration, we thank you for your sacrificial love, comfort and obedience:

Rev. Billy Joe Daughtery, Rev. Kenneth Hagin Jr., Rev. Kenneth Copeland, Rev. Richard Roberts, Rev. Eastman Curtis and Rev. Dave Williams.

Special thanks come from our hearts to Richard and Lindsay Roberts and to all of our loving family members for standing with us and loving Gabrielle so deeply.

To Tracey Jacobs, "Nanny," who became a sister to Gabrielle by choice and loved her beyond all measure, we love you like a daughter.

To our dear friends, Eastman and Angel Curtis, we thank you for being instrumental in taking us out of captivity. Your joy brought us strength. And to Destiny Church for the repeated meals that sustained us physically.

To Grandpa Glenn and Miss Dee (Simmons), we extend our deepest gratitude not only for your financial and spiritual support but also for taking time out of your worldwide business schedule to sit and color with a six-year-old girl.

To Rev. Rocky and Jodi Bezet and Rev. Ron and Belinda Clark, we say thank you for the wonderful wahoo parties as well as everything else you have done. Wahoo!

To Mel and Desiree Ayres and Rev. Ron and Melody Villar, we say thank you for the fashion show and "auction of all auctions" you held for Gabrielle, and for loving us through the toughest year of our lives.

To Sara Baty and Megan Hull, Gabrielle's faithful friends, we love you for never getting weary of coming to visit and play with her.

To Rev. Fred and Valerie Bennett, who loved us through the good times and the bad times, we want you to know how happy Gabrielle was when she got to visit Uncle Fred and Aunt Valerie. On her last ministry trip she said, "I'm so glad I got to come and see Pastor Fred and Valerie again."

To Louis Waller, Gabrielle's lemon-pound-cake-baking security guard and special friend, we dearly appreciate how you stayed and took care of her through the night until she was placed in her final resting place.

Special thanks to the medical professionals who did all they could for Gabrielle: Dr. Ritze, Dr. Lee, and the staff at the Cancer Treatment Center of America—from Joe Gagliardia and CEO Dick Stephenson to the parking attendants, and especially Lori Maynard in the laboratory and Karen Gilbert, the therapist who came to our home.

To Nootsie Stricklin, thank you for your efforts in the last months to help us find special ways to make Gabrielle more comfortable.

To the researchers at the Burzynski Clinic we extend our appreciation for your efforts in trying to find a cure for this despicable disease but implore you to find compassion in this field of life and death.

To all of the worldwide ministries that loved and supported us—Richard and Lindsay Roberts, Oral and

Evelyn Roberts, Billy Joe and Sharon Daugherty, Benny and Suzanne Hinn, Pat Robertson and the 700 Club, Kenneth and Gloria Copeland, Kenneth and Lynette Hagin, Eastman and Angel Curtis, Jesse and Cathy Duplantis, Jan and Paul Crouch and the TBN family, Matt and Laurie Crouch, Marcus and Joni Lamb and the Daystar family, Terry Law, Dave and Mary Jo Williams, Vicki Jamison-Peterson (just to name a few)—we thank you for stopping and taking the time for one little girl. Because of your great calling, you minister to the multitudes; but, just like Jesus, you took the time for one. We don't have enough paper to thank all of you, but you know who you are. So do Gabrielle and God!

To the people who made her home-going party so beautiful: Victory Christian Center, the ORU staff, all the volunteers and helpers and the Tulsa Police Department.

To Joe and Eunice Moore, owners of the Moore Funeral Home, who provided Gabrielle's home-going as a gift, we want you to know that the impact you made on our lives is everlasting.

To the Memorial Park Cemetery that blessed Gabrielle with her final earthly place, you truly were the beginning of the restoration process for our family.

To all of the participants in the Gabrielle Christian Salem Dormitory Memorial Fund at Oral Roberts University, we thank you for joining us in this "living" memorial to Gabrielle. Women will be coming to "Gabrielle's House" for many years and helping to fulfill her destiny to preach the Gospel in all the nations of the world.

To all of the donors and organizations that gave to Gabrielle's medical fund, we extend our thanks and appreciation. You planted good seed in fertile ground, and we pray a multiplication of blessings upon you.

Ackerman Church of Christ

Mr. & Mrs. Jon Nash

Stephanie Cantees

Pastor & Mrs. Mel Ayres
In His Presence Church

Mr. & Mrs. Daniel Slack

Amber Miloszewski

Joyce Bennett & Jelaine Luke

Charles Capps Ministries, Inc.

Christopher Scott Robbings

Pastor & Mrs. Rocky Bezet
Cornerstone Church of Zachary, Inc.

Karen Hofer

Jessie Lea Hughes

Peace In The Valley Church

Foreword

My Little Chick-a-Dee
by Patricia (Salem) White

What an honor and privilege it is to tell you about my granddaughter, Gabrielle Christian Salem. I called her my "little chick-a-dee!"

About the time Cheryl was nearing completion of her pregnancy with Gabrielle, Little Harry III asked me to watch him in his new adventure called rollerblading. Not having encountered this before, I thought, *Why not?*

Well, he rollerbladed and I watched, until he hit an area of the driveway that was beyond his expertise and came to a crashing halt. By getting between him and the concrete, I was successful in breaking his fall. But *breaking* is the important word. He was unharmed. However, I broke my collarbone and immediately was taken to the doctor for all the necessary medical attention.

In the midst of all the excitement, I was sent to bed, and Cheryl was sent to the hospital in labor with Gabrielle. After the baby was born and all was well, Harry and Cheryl brought her to see me on their way home from the hospital. I knew when I saw my little granddaughter's face that she was someone very special. Even at two days old, her face lit up as if someone had turned on the electricity.

With a smile that could capture the hardest of hearts, Gabrielle was sweet, funny and mischievous. As she grew in years, her stature remained tiny in comparison to her two older brothers. But in no way did that hinder her from thinking that she, in fact, was in charge!

I always had dates with her brothers, Harry III and Roman, on Friday and Saturday nights. I remember one Friday night so very well. Gabrielle was only three years old, and she decided she, too, wanted a date. Standing at the door, she stamped her little foot and said, "I never get to go; I never get to go; I never get to go!"

Finally, I said to the boys, "Let's just take her for a few hours. When it gets dark, she will want to go home."

She got into the car, sat between her brothers and never stopped chattering until we arrived at my house. When one of the boys asked her to be quiet for a moment, her response was "typical Gabrielle" as she said, "Well, you invited me to go, and now you want me to be quiet. If I get to go, I get to talk!" That established a pattern that was never broken from that day forward.

Gabrielle was a child on a mission for God, and she knew it. She loved to sing for the Lord. Her favorite song was "I'm Old Enough To Praise the Lord," and praising the Lord was something she did constantly. She loved to pray, and she did it well. When she touched you, you knew you had felt the power of God.

One thing I shall never forget is her character—the essence of Gabrielle. It happened all throughout her illness: Going through her trial, she demonstrated something I've rarely seen in all my lifetime. She had an uncanny ability to make you comfortable despite her own personal discomfort. She never complained and never asked, "Why me?" She was always happy, always singing, always drawing beautiful pictures of the sun, bees and butterflies.

My sixty-ninth birthday party was a perfect example of Gabrielle's unselfishness. She had been experiencing some very difficult physical problems and had not been out of bed for some time. But she asked me one day if I would like her to plan my birthday party. I said I would just be delighted. She said she wanted to take me to the Cracker Barrel® Restaurant and proceeded to tell me what to wear. She said we would eat chicken and dumplings, because it was her favorite, and she knew I would just love it. She was so right! It was my most memorable and happiest birthday yet. And I know it always will be.

Gabrielle was a perfect example of unconditional love. She never knew a stranger; everyone was her *new, very best friend.* I truly believe she accomplished more in six-and-one-half years than most people do in seventy-five years. I know in my own life, I am striving more for excellence in everything I do because of her living example of love. She showed the love of Christ in her beautiful face. The value of her smile, her laughter and her singing—from the day she came into my life until the morning the Lord Jesus ushered her into her heavenly home—can never be measured in earthly terms.

Her favorite saying was "Ya come to my house?" She always ended her conversation with me in this manner. If I wasn't at home, she left a message on my answering machine, and she meant it as an invitation from the bottom of her heart.

"Yes, Gabrielle, when I finish my work here, I promise I *am* coming to your house!"

Introduction:

Morning Will Come and the Son Will Shine Again!

by Harry Salem

It was 4:00 A.M. that dark night of November 24, 1999, when for the first time in my life I seriously doubted that the sun would ever shine again. It wasn't that I feared the end of the world had come or that Y2K had arrived early. The reason I felt the darkness so intensely was that less than twenty-four hours earlier I had watched the light of my life pass from this world to the next. Gabrielle Christian Salem, our precious six-year-old daughter, had walked out of our bedroom into the arms of Jesus and gone on before us. Our family would never be the same again. The light of her presence and the joy that lit up the room when she was there was now only a memory.

As I sat in the darkness of our bedroom trying to comprehend the reality of Gabrielle's passing, I wondered if the emptiness and pain Cheryl and the boys and I were feeling would ever go away. Much of the drama of the past year had taken place right in this room with Gabrielle in our bed, and the boys sleeping on the floor at the foot of the bed. She never left our sides. Now we were facing the deepest pain a family ever experiences—the death of a child.

I don't know why I reached over and flipped on the TV at such a time, but I was blessed when I saw Jan Crouch on TBN talking with her son and daughter-in-law, Matt and Laurie Crouch, about Gabrielle and her home-going. The words of comfort and concern they spoke were blessed assurance of God's grace.

Jan shared a Scripture that spoke to my heart at that moment:

> *The good men perish; the godly die before their time, and no one seems to care or wonder why. No one seems to realize that God is taking them away from evil days ahead. For the godly who die shall rest in peace.*
>
> ISAIAH 57:1,2 TLB

She went on to say this: "We may not understand why Gabrielle was taken home, but perfect healing is there. And our little angel is running around on streets of gold, just absolutely, perfectly whole. Though we are grieving, the Holy Spirit is our Comforter; and we have the assurance that we will one day see this precious angel again in heaven. We don't always understand everything, but God's plans are perfect. Why would anyone not want to know the

Lord through a time like this? Instead of blaming, we fall in His arms and say, 'Your ways are perfect.'"

Laurie Crouch said, "I think about Cheryl, and as a mother here's something that has helped me through some things. Our children love to go to Disneyland, and they know they have to have a ticket to get in. They want to hold the ticket, but as parents we know they might lose it. So we hold the ticket until we get up to the gate and then give them their tickets to be able to get in. That is how God's grace works. His grace is always there, but He holds the ticket and hands it to us when we need it to get through a trial. Harry and Cheryl will know God in a way that I hopefully never will. They will know a peace and a blessed assurance of God's grace."

As daylight began to creep into the room, I looked out the window. Just then the Lord spoke to my hurting heart and said, *Yes, you are in mourning and you are numb, but just as the sun is shining through the window, morning is coming. The Son will come out in the morning and shine through all of you.*

This book was born in my spirit at that precise moment. Yes, we were in mourning, but God did not mean for us to stay there. Grief is real, and it is a necessary process toward restoration. What believers must understand is that God doesn't mean for us to mourn the way the world mourns— that is "without hope," as it says in this Scripture:

> *Now also we would not have you ignorant, brethren, about those who fall asleep [in death], that you may not grieve [for them] as the rest do who have no hope [beyond the grave].*

1 THESSALONIANS 4:13 AMP

We know where Gabrielle is, and we rejoice that she is in the arms of Jesus. Do we still feel the pain of being separated from her? Absolutely. It is more painful than anyone can ever imagine. Does the pain ever go away? No, but it moves further away with time. Have we seen the Son shine out of the midst of the trial? Yes, we have seen more salvations and miracles in our services than we ever saw before her passing. Testimonies continue to pour in from all over the world of how Gabrielle has touched and changed people's lives.

As God spoke to me, I knew the title of this book would be *From Mourning to Morning*. While sharing this revelation with Cheryl, we realized the only difference between those two words is the letter "u." *You* have to make a decision whether you want to move out of mourning and see the glory of the Son each morning, because there is an appointed time for restoration. *You* have to choose whether to be a professional mourner sitting by the grave, or to throw off the grave clothes and let the Son shine out of your life so others can find their way to Him.

And so it was for our family. We chose to trust in God and His promises even when it took us through the valley of the shadow of death. We chose to let the light of God shine through us when we didn't feel like letting it shine.

The nightmarish hell of 1999 came and went. Along with it, death came and went. But we determined in our hearts that, although grief came, we weren't going to let it stay. Where the enemy had tried to keep us captive and isolated, we pushed on through, declaring victory.

When the new millennium dawned, we were back on track ministering in churches that we had to move from our schedule the previous year due to Gabrielle's illness. We were preaching, singing and experiencing the anointing and glimpses of God's glory as we never had before!

Even after Gabrielle's death, the devil didn't walk away. He kept up the attack, this time coming against Cheryl's body. Every five to seven days, she was waking up sick. No matter how much we prayed and spoke the Word over her, the symptoms persisted. On Wednesday, February 23, 2000—exactly three months after Gabrielle graduated to heaven—Cheryl went into surgery to have a malignant tumor removed from her colon, along with eleven inches of colon and eighteen lymph nodes. Only one lymph node had any cancer cells, and Cheryl has been given a clean bill of health. We praise God that she is healed and completely made whole by the blood of the Lamb.

This war is not over. It has only begun. It may appear that Gabrielle was a casualty of war, but she has already received the victor's crown of life, and we rejoice because of it. The devil lost, even though he thought he won. He lost again when he tried to take Cheryl's life. We have not slowed down at all, because the calling of this family is still for the appointed time—and the time is NOW! God will not deceive or disappoint us. We have taken ground in the spirit realm, and we are not willing to give it up!

Restoration is the word from God for this hour. We have and are still shouting, "Restore!" for our family, our health and our finances. If you have ever felt robbed, snared, hidden, bound or as though you were being attacked like prey, then we want you to stand up and shout, "Restore!" with us. That is why we have written this book: so you can learn how to walk *through* the tragedies and trials of life, as we have, and find victory, peace and, yes, even joy on the other side.

Cheryl and I have opened our hearts to you in this book, sharing both our most intimate, private pain and the powerful revelations God revealed to us in the midst of it, because we want you to be equipped for battle *before* the enemy strikes. We have also inserted some of the testimonies and words of wisdom we received from numerous men and women of God who knew and loved Gabrielle. We want you to know God is the God of restoration, as it says in this Scripture:

> *For the vision is yet for an appointed time and it hastens to the end [fulfillment]; it will not deceive or disappoint. Though it tarry, wait [earnestly] for it, because it will surely come; it will not be behindhand on its appointed day.*

> HABAKKUK 2:3 AMP

Healing restoration has come and is still coming for us, and it will surely come for you, too. It is time to shout, "Restore!" It's our right! It's our voice of triumph! Let it be yours as well. No matter how dark the night seems to be, morning *will* come and the Son will shine again!

When the World Turns Upside Down

by Cheryl Salem

January 11, 1999, was the day our world turned upside down. It was the day our rapturous life as a traveling ministry family became a living, hellish nightmare, when doctors informed us that our precious, five-year-old daughter, Gabrielle, had an inoperable brain tumor and that she would be gone in two months. How could this be? Our minds were reeling with such an evil report, and our hearts were broken.

An Incredible Year

We had just finished the most incredible year of our lives, ministering the power of God as a family in over 250 churches, and we looked forward with great anticipation to the New Year. The entire traveling schedule was already set on the calendar, and we were ready to take God's kingdom further than we had ever taken it before. We had been speaking the Word, praying in the Spirit, pleading the blood of Jesus over each one of our family members and ministry and had begun to see positive effects from it all.

During the 1998 Christmas holidays while visiting my family in Mississippi, Gabrielle had started having terrible nightmares. She would wake up screaming at the top of her lungs, and no matter what we did, nothing would calm her. For no explainable reason, night terrors plagued her night after night.

About a week later, after returning home, we noticed that her eyes were not moving properly. She was turning her entire head to look at something instead of moving her eyes to the left or the right. When I tried to get her to follow my finger with her eyes, she couldn't do it. We called our family physician and explained her symptoms. He suggested we see an ophthalmologist.

The ophthalmologist examined our precious gift from God and knew immediately something was seriously wrong. Harry knew before I did just how serious it was. The ophthalmologist asked him to step out of the room and said, "This is what is called 'doll's eyes,' and it is generally caused by pressure on the brain." He couldn't give Harry any definitive diagnosis, but he immediately ordered an MRI and called a specialist.

Crushed, but Not Without Hope

We rushed Gabrielle to the hospital for the MRI, and again the man who did the scan took Harry aside and said, "Generally the doctors tell you this, but I'm not going to put you through a long wait until morning. I saw something in the brain stem, and it's not good."

Harry had to tell me what we were facing. We were crushed, but not without hope.

The next morning we met with the radiologist at the hospital, and she gave us the devastating report. She said, "It is a malignant tumor known as a glioma in the brain stem, and it is inoperable. It is one of the most aggressive types of tumors, and your daughter has two months, maybe six, to live."

We later learned that this type of tumor occurs almost exclusively in children between the ages of four and six. They are fast growing and, barring a miracle from God, always fatal.

Mobilized for Prayer

We took Gabrielle and went directly to Richard and Lindsay Roberts' home. (Lindsay is Harry's sister.) Richard called his father and mother, Oral and Evelyn, and we prayed with them over the phone. We'd had the wind knocked out of us by this evil report, but we knew it was not from God. Immediately, we began to regroup and start warring in the spiritual realm for our daughter's life. We called other pastor/ministry friends and mobilized prayer warriors everywhere we could.

We decided to minister as scheduled on Richard Roberts' television program that evening. We wanted to give immediately out of our pain and hurt to continue to fight for others, as we would want them to fight for us!

Researching the Options

We knew we had to do everything possible in the natural realm as well, in order to examine all the options for Gabrielle. Her reports were sent to St. Jude's Children's Hospital in Memphis, Tennessee, and the specialist asked for another MRI to be done. After examining all the scans and reports, he called back, confirmed the diagnosis and said, "I'm sorry. There is nothing we can do," and abruptly hung up.

We contacted one of the leading neurosurgeons at Mt. Sinai Hospital in New York City who is one of the few surgeons in the world skilled in operating on brain stem tumors. He reviewed all of the scans and reports and set up a conference call for us with him and two other specialists in New York. He was very caring and gracious, but said there was nothing he could do or recommend that would save our little girl.

We had one other option to consider, a physician in Houston, Texas, who operates a clinic for the treatment of brain tumors using an experimental treatment methodology that is considered to be alternative medicine. When all forms of traditional medicine had failed, this physician had successfully treated many brain tumor cases. We prayed and felt led by the Lord to pursue this course of treatment.

Going on for God

Harry and I purposed in our hearts that we would do everything we could for Gabrielle *and* continue on with our family ministry. The devil was not going to stop what God had called and ordained us to do for His kingdom. We continued our ministry schedule on TV and in churches as best we were able.

The devil was not going to stop what God had called and ordained us to do for His kingdom.

During the twenty years we have been in full-time ministry, we have faced many adversities. We lost a son to a miscarriage; and when I was pregnant with our fourth baby, I hemorrhaged so badly that the doctors told me the baby was gone. I refused to believe their report, and after spending the next seven months in bed, Gabrielle Christian Salem was born, completely whole and healthy. We then faced months of sleepless nights after she was diagnosed with sleep apnea. In 1994 depression tried to destroy me; an eighteen-month battle ensued, until I was totally healed.

We faced each challenge with great strength from Jesus, knowing that He *always* honors His Word, no matter how long or how hard the battle. These were times of great pressurization, which the Holy Spirit used to grow us and mature us in the Spirit realm. Each time we came out stronger, more equipped for the next battle and, ultimately, the next victory.

We faced each challenge with great strength from Jesus, knowing that He always honors His Word, no matter how long or how hard the battle.

Through all of this we had learned the power of the spoken Word of God. It transformed our family and saved our lives. This battle would be no different than any other. We knew what to do when the enemy attacked.

Battle Readiness

One of the first things we have learned about warfare is to call an evil report just what it is and recognize from where it comes. In our case, we didn't call it a "diagnosis." It was an evil report, and it came from the devil, not from God. Too many times, people blame God instead of the true culprit, Satan.

Just because the devil brings an evil report doesn't mean you have to receive it. God's Word is very clear about this, as we can read here:

Therefore submit to God. Resist the devil and he will flee from you.

JAMES 4:7,8 NKJV

A radiologist told us we were in denial regarding Gabrielle's diagnosis. We said to her, "That's right. We *are* in denial. We deny the devil any right to do this. We deny this disease any right to live in our daughter. We deny this thing any right to come near our household. Absolutely, we are in denial!"

Too many times, people blame God instead of the true culprit, Satan.

God's Word is true, and if you are submitted to God and resist the devil, he *will* flee. The Scripture doesn't say he *might* flee. It says he *will* flee. He can't stick around, and he can't steal your ground when you stand firm in the Word.

If Satan knocked on your door, would you answer it and let him come in? Some people fearfully say, "Oh, it's Satan! What do I do? Well, come on in and have a cup of coffee until I figure out what to do." They open the door and let arthritis come in the house and sit down as though it were their friend.

Have you ever said something like this: "*My* arthritis sure is bothering me today"? It's not yours. It's Satan's. I don't care if its been hanging around for twenty years—it still isn't yours. Sickness is a squatter, and you have every right to throw it off your land.

The Word: A Defensive and an Offensive Weapon

When we heard the evil report regarding Gabrielle, the only defense we had was the Word of God. We had to resist the devil and this evil report. We had to speak what we know to be true and not what we were told or what we were seeing.

"Take the Word like a prescription. Follow the directions, do not miss a dose and continue until health has returned in full."

The Word of God is not just a defensive weapon, as a shield. It is also an offensive weapon, as a sword. His shield protects us, and His sword defeats and cuts asunder the enemy and all his cohorts. Using the Word of God against the devil is how we truly resist him!

As a family we immediately began to speak the Word of God concerning healing over Gabrielle. As difficult as it was, we knew it was absolutely necessary to achieve the desired result we were after: *healing!* Harry would say over and over, "I'm not questioning God when it comes to Gabrielle's healing; I'm counting on it!"

Write It Out and Make It Plain

The Lord instructed us to write out His Word so we could insert Gabrielle's or anyone else's name into it. In this way we could really pray every Word out loud for Gabrielle, and other people as well. As we did this, we began to compile every Scripture we knew on healing. We pulled out all of our old Bibles to collect the healing Scriptures we had highlighted and used at different times in our lives. We studied the Scriptures and prayed for more revelation. It was as if the Lord was saying, "Take the Word like a prescription. Follow the directions. Do not miss a dose, and continue until health has returned in full."

When your world turns upside down for whatever reason, the Word of God is the only thing that doesn't change and can't be shaken.

This study process resulted in creating a new series of books titled *Speak the Word Over Your Family for....* The first two editions, *for Healing* and *for Salvation*, are already in print, and more will soon follow. We have done this because we know that when your world turns upside down for whatever reason, the Word of God is the only thing that doesn't change and can't be shaken.

The Power of the Spoken Word

Speaking the Word out loud changes our futures, our families, our marriages and our hopes. Speaking the Word gives us faith and confidence that God *does* what He *says* He will do. We activate His Word by praying it into the atmosphere. Our job is to speak out of our mouths what God says, and it is God's job to perform His Word. He sends His messengers to perform what we say, *when we say what He says!*

Speaking the Word out loud changes our futures, our families, our marriages and our hopes.

If your world has turned upside down, don't open the door to Satan. If you or someone you love has received an evil report, don't sign for it. It doesn't belong to you. Speak the Word daily over every evil circumstance and situation and resist the devil at every turn. Take your Jesus medicine every day and *believe* God no matter what is happening around you. Stop just talking about your family or circumstances and start covering them with God's Word today.

Sunshine Girl

by Carrie (Prewitt) McAdams

Gabrielle was the bravest little girl I have ever known. In all she went through, she never fussed; she never complained; she never asked, "Why me?"

She was always so sweet about everything. In fact, no matter how she felt, she always wanted to do something for somebody else. She was always drawing a picture for someone to make them happy.

She would say, "Let me draw a picture for you." In every picture she drew flowers, butterflies, rainbows, bees, happy faces and sunshine—everything that would make you smile. She was my "sunshine" girl.

Gabrielle brought joy and happiness to everyone she met. She made me proud to be her Granny.

Choosing Life

by Harry Salem

Have you ever noticed that even in the midst of turmoil, life goes on? Day turns into night, and night turns into day. It is simply how you choose to respond to the turmoil that makes any difference at all. The devil's evil report spoke of death, but we chose abundant life in Christ for Gabrielle, our family and our ministry. We declared up front that the enemy was not going to distract us with the problem, because we were focusing on The Solution—Jesus Christ.

The Testing Begins

The weekend after receiving the doctors' reports, the Salem family ministered Friday, Saturday and Sunday in

Texas. Monday morning we drove to Houston, where Gabrielle would begin treatment at the alternative medicine clinic. Our mobile phone never stopped ringing as word of our impending battle spread through Christian circles. Prayers and words of encouragement poured in as the body of Christ stood in the gap and upheld our arms, as Aaron and Hur did for Moses. (Ex. 17:12.)

The first step in Gabrielle's medical treatment process was having a catheter port inserted in her chest to receive the numerous intravenous medications and to facilitate numerous blood drawings. It was a horribly traumatic experience for everyone, as Gabrielle had a terrible reaction to the anesthetic. From that point on, Gabrielle carried a portable IV pump, weighing almost fifteen pounds, in a little Barbie backpack everywhere she went, day and night. It was as if it became a part of her, and she took it in stride.

Over the course of almost a month, we stayed in Houston receiving hours of instruction regarding the medical treatment process. Cheryl and Tracey, a young lady who has been with us and helped us in many capacities for over ten years and is almost a daughter to us, learned how to prepare and administer the intravenous solutions, how to care for the catheter port, how to draw blood and how to record all the vital information needed on a daily basis. They were the ones who would be doing all of the hands-on care for Gabrielle.

I stayed with Gabrielle and took her to her daily doctor's visits while Cheryl and Tracey went to their training sessions. My mom was there to stay with the boys.

I remember that I didn't change my clothes for almost a week. I couldn't eat anything and lost thirty-five pounds during that month.

Traveling Hospital

When we left Houston, our motor coach was like a traveling hospital. We continued traveling and ministering through the next several months. We settled into a routine, each contributing what he or she could to the process of caring for Gabrielle's and each other's needs. At each destination we would find a hotel, and Tracy would go in to prepare the rooms, making sure they were antiseptically clean and arranged properly, while Cheryl got ready to move Gabrielle in. Tracy usually prepared the IV bags each day, and Cheryl did the hands-on care of administering the medications, flushing the IV port and drawing blood.

The boys and I would carry in all of the necessary medical equipment and supplies to set up the hotel rooms. Then I would carry Gabrielle out of the motor coach and place her in a special chair I had built on wheels to transport her in and out of the house, the hotel or anywhere else we went. After getting Gabrielle settled in the hotel, I would unload all of our suitcases and personal items. It was quite an operation.

Beating the Clock

Since it was necessary to draw blood and have it tested at least three times a week, at each destination I had to find a laboratory in a hospital, clinic or independent facility that could process the blood. Cheryl and I agreed that we would not subject Gabrielle to being taken in and out of dozens of hospitals for the blood draws, so Cheryl drew the blood either in the motor coach or in the hotel room. Then I had a window of time—one hour—to get it to the lab to be processed. It didn't matter if it was 5:30 in the morning; I had to find a place to take it. I learned my way around many cities and around the bureaucracies of the health care world.

I wasn't much good with needles or giving medicine, so I did whatever else I could do. Sometimes when Cheryl was trying to draw blood she couldn't get it to flow, so I would have to help find the veins in Gabrielle's little chest and roll her around while Cheryl handled the needle, being careful not to make the catheter collapse. There were times we were all soaked with perspiration from the stress by the time we were finished, but we managed. A key that carried us through the tough times was doing what we had to do day-by-day and claiming victory for that day alone.

A key that carried us through the tough times was doing what we had to do day-by-day and claiming victory for that day alone.

Gabrielle had to drink literally gallons of water to flush the medication and saline solutions through her system, which meant many, many potty episodes. I emptied the potty, took out the trash, did the grocery shopping for all organic and natural foods and helped with the cooking. Some of the time my mom traveled with us, and she helped with the boys, the cooking and laundry, which was a blessing.

Big Brothers–Faithful Servants

Cheryl and I are so proud of the way our boys helped Gabrielle and helped us throughout Gabrielle's illness. They were troopers. It was an unwritten, unspoken thing. We never had to talk with them about it. They just did it.

She had to be on a low-salt diet, and so we all ate what she ate. That meant no more fast food. For months we ate bland chicken and organic vegetables. The boys never complained once. If Gabrielle didn't like something, they would convince her it was good. At one point she had to take a liquid steroid, and she didn't want to take it. The boys came in and said, "We'll try it first." It tasted horrible, but the boys bravely kept happy faces as they tasted it. She looked at them and said, "Well, then, you take it! I'm not taking it!"

True Grit

They went with us to the clinic and sat with her, holding her hand and bringing her dolls. One day she was feeling really bad, and she kept smacking Roman. He came out of the room just gritting his teeth. That showed me his stamina and self-restraint. It was remarkable for a nine-year-old boy to just bite his tongue and take it.

The sacrifices they made were great, but they never complained. It was Roman's birthday the day we found out Gabrielle had the tumor. They never questioned why they had to do things or said, "I won't do it," or "I'm not going."

The boys used the little chair I built to transport Gabrielle into and out of the motor coach and made it into a journey. They said, "Okay, Gabrielle, we're going on a roller coaster." They made it fun, and they all laughed. Instead of targeting in on the affliction, they decided to make something fun out of this bad situation. It didn't matter if it was cleaning the potty, getting up at 4 A.M. to take the blood draws, or getting up through the night

Instead of targeting in on the affliction, they decided to make something fun out of this bad situation.

because she was vomiting, they never ran out of the room. They stayed right there, patting her on the back and comforting her.

They would make her eggs, bacon and toast into a smiley face and carry it up to her in the morning. Every meal was brought up to her room. They watched movie after movie with her, over and over and over.

Whenever Little Harry went out, he always came back with something in his hand for her. He was given a $500 honorarium at Rhema Bible Church for speaking to the youth, and I asked what he was going to do with it. He said, "I'm going to buy sister that Game Boy®." He bought her a purple Game Boy with a pink Barbie® disc, using his own money. She saw a Barbie airplane on TV, and he called his aunt to come take him to the store so he could buy it for her. That was his way of keeping her happy.

They would sit for hours with her and just color, swapping pictures as they worked. They let her just drench them with the Super Soaker. You know what it is like to get a remote control out of a little boy's hand, but she was allowed to pick what she wanted to watch. They never said anything to her about her weight as her body reacted to the steroids; and they always kept her away from the mirrors, because she didn't like to look in them.

Rose-colored Glasses

One of the first things we said to Gabrielle was "You're going through this so your eyes will work." The boys got her big glasses with no glass in them so she would have glasses. They just did the little things kids do for other kids.

Everything that they did revolved around Gabrielle. It wasn't about what they did or didn't do that year. Roman didn't play baseball that year and never spent the night with anyone. If someone came to the house, Roman made sure they washed their hands and used the liquid sanitizer to keep everything antiseptically clean. It was as if they were thirty-five-year-old men.

Roman slept at the foot of her bed every night, and Harry was in his room praying. He was the hidden intercessor, praying and speaking the Word over her. To this day, Roman still prays a prayer covering over his sister.

Stamina That Never Quit

It amazed Cheryl and me that they never tired of doing the same thing over and over for eleven months. They never sighed or moaned, "Do I have to pray again? Do I have to do this? Do I have to go get this?"

Other children got tired of it. They quit coming over or quit coloring. We didn't blame them. Most children don't have a long attention span. It amazed us that a nine- and a thirteen-year-old boy did not tire of the same rote thing every day in taking care of her and in making her feel better and lifting her spirits.

They never said, "I want to do my own thing." We were tired physically, so I kept expecting them to say, "Do I have to go in there and color today?" But never once did they say it. It showed their stamina and faith. They never gave up.

The boys included her in everything—even in watching the fireworks. Harry wanted to blow firecrackers off in her bedroom because she couldn't come outside. We derived a way to get her to the window. One fellow sent us rockets to build, and I didn't build them right. We went outside to shoot them off and that first rocket went up and then did a ninety-degree turn and took off chasing me down the backyard. She was in the window watching and laughing.

They always stood by her and stayed with her. They didn't let anybody come between them or let anybody hurt her. They watched over her and did all the things she liked to do, day after day after day. That's something really special. They used the time that they had to be with her.

The Princess Never Missed a Beat!

Because of the large doses of steroids she was on, Gabrielle's weight ballooned from thirty-seven pounds to ninety-seven pounds. She was only five years old. It was difficult to find clothes that would fit. One morning Gabrielle seemed upset about something. I asked her what the problem was, and in her own little way she let me know that she was embarrassed because none of her clothes fit. Immediately, I made a trip to Wal-Mart and returned with pink, purple, yellow and blue pants and matching shirts and socks, bows for her hair and little pocketbooks. She liked everything to match, and we did everything we could to keep her spirits up. Eventually, we had to dress her in multi-colored T-shirts that we had to cut off and hem. In spite of all this, our beautiful little princess who loved frilly dresses never missed a beat and continued to sing and minister in meetings as often as she could.

Unstoppable Anointing

While we were in Houston at the clinic, Dr. Oral Roberts was there to pray for Pastor John Osteen, who was very ill at the time. We asked Oral to come and pray over Gabrielle. Instead, Gabrielle insisted on praying for Oral. He said there was more anointing flowing out of her than he had ever experienced from a child. In his words, she was unstoppable! The following Monday, Oral suffered a heart attack himself but recovered completely.

That same week, Pastor Osteen went on to be with the Lord. Richard and Lindsay Roberts attended his home-going celebration, and the first thing Dodie Osteen said to them was "How's Gabrielle?" Gabrielle was on people's hearts no matter what state of mind they were in. Oral said it was amazing to him that we didn't have a national television ministry and yet everywhere he went the first thing people asked him, before anything else, was "How's Gabrielle?"

The Longest Road

As Cheryl shared in chapter 1, we prayed the pure Word of God over Gabrielle every day. We sang and played praise and worship music constantly to keep her and ourselves built up. At times it seemed like the longest road. To be honest, there were days and opportunities that made us all want to quit, but there is no quitting when it comes to spiritual warfare.

We are designed by God to always win if we just stick with it until the victory comes from the supernatural to the natural realm.

We are designed by God to *always* win if we just stick with it until the victory comes from the supernatural to the natural realm. If we resist the devil, the unseen realm will literally swallow up the seen realm. If the *seen* does not line up with God's Word, then we have a biblical right to believe God for the seen to be swallowed up by the *unseen!*

His Word Never Changes

We believed God no matter what report the doctors gave us. We believed God no matter what the symptoms were. We believed God no matter what we felt. *We believed God!* Months passed, but time did not change the Word of God. It was still true. Each month we believed and expected the report of man to line up with the report of the Lord.

When Gabrielle had been in Cheryl's womb and the doctors had said she'd miscarried, Cheryl had refused to believe the evil report. She'd spoken Psalm 118:17 over herself and the baby in her womb: "This baby will live and not die and declare the works of the Lord in his/her life." We spoke this same Word over her throughout this battle. We chose life in the face of every evil report!

Worldwide Prayer

Many have said Gabrielle was the most prayed for little girl in the world. Not only were we speaking the Word and believing God for her healing, but partners of the Oral Roberts and Richard Roberts Ministries, Pat Robertson and the 700 Club, tens of thousands of people in Benny Hinn's crusades, TBN and their prayer partners, Marcus and Joni Lamb and the Daystar audiences, thousands of churches and cell groups and countless people all over the world, faxed, called and wrote numerous letters to tell us that they were praying. Even some monks in Europe sent faxes telling us that they were praying for Gabrielle. Children from churches and schools sent banners and cards they had signed.

Each month her symptoms were worse, but our faith never wavered. One of the greatest promises we clung to is in this Scripture:

> *God is not a man, that He should tell or act a lie, neither the son of man, that He should feel repentance or compunction [for what He has promised]. Has He said and shall He not do it? Or has He spoken and shall He not make it good?*
>
> NUMBERS 23:19 AMP

God Alone Is God

After meditating on this Scripture for weeks, Cheryl was drawn to the words "God is not a man..." Those words played over and over in her spirit. She finally received the full revelation of what God wanted her to see: *God is not a man! He is God and God alone!*

These are God's promises, and He does not lie. He performs what He says when we say what He says!

We had to stop looking at God as we look to people to keep their word. God is God, and He does not lie. He does not promise something and then not keep that promise. That is why, as you speak the Word over yourself and your family for healing, you must remember these are God's promises and He does not lie. He performs what He says when *we say what He says!*

Death Is Not the Healer

God showed us so many revelations and one was that many times people make "death" the healer. God continued to say to us, *I am the Lord that heals Gabrielle. You will have no other God's before Me.*

We refused to let "death" be Gabrielle's healer, because we realized this is one of Satan's greatest deceptions. When death becomes a healer in our minds, then death becomes a god. We must hold our ground, and if healing comes in crossing over to the other side instead of healing on earth, we must be very careful not to fall into the mental trap of calling "death" the healer. Jesus is the healer.

Graduation Day

At 7:05 A.M. on November 23, 1999, Gabrielle Christian crossed over. She graduated to heaven. She went beyond the veil, but death did not take her. Death did not heal her. We walked her as far as we could on this side through the valley of the shadow of death.

This was another revelation God gave us. The valley of the shadow of death is on this side of the heavenly realm. Cheryl said it must be because there are no shadows in heaven. Once a believer steps beyond this earthly realm, there is no valley to cross: He or she is instantly in the presence of the Lord. The heavenly realm is that close.

The valley of the shadow of death is on this side of the heavenly realm.

The Angels Came

Cheryl and I had been taking turns sitting up with Gabrielle at night. We'd known the end was near. Cheryl had been with her that last night and had seen the angels come down the hall for Gabrielle three times. Each time she said, "Not now. Go back. I'm not ready yet." Three times they came and backed off. I came into the room early that morning of November 23, and at 6:55 A.M. Cheryl said to me, "I'm so sleepy. I have to lay my head down for just five minutes." Instantly, she fell into a deep sleep.

As I was watching Gabrielle, she opened her eyes and started blowing kisses. I don't know if she was looking at me, or if she saw Jesus in heaven. Then I felt a presence enter our bedroom. It was not an angel, nor was it a spirit of death. The Man Himself—Jesus—showed up. There was an indescribable stillness and peace, as it is just before an earthquake when the atmosphere is so completely still that even the birds stop chirping.

Then I heard myself say, "There she goes." Before I finished saying the word "goes," the words "Here she comes" came out of His mouth. "There she…Here she comes." It was that quick. We didn't lose her. He got her! She ran toward her healing so quickly that she just left her earthly shell behind. Her natural container, or body, couldn't keep up with her supernatural healing. Jesus remained the healer, not death.

When Gabrielle had been born, I'd looked at her and said, "Someday, little girl, you're going to break my heart." I was referring to the day I would walk her down the aisle and give her over to another man—her husband, I thought. I just knew that no man would be worthy of her. I never expected that I would be handing her over at only six years of age to The Man—the only Man Daddy could deem worthy of his precious daughter, the One to whom the angels in heaven bow down and cry, "Worthy, worthy, worthy is the Lamb!"

What more could a daddy ask, but that his daughter be in the loving arms of the worthy Lamb of God for eternity?

We spoke life over and over for Gabrielle, and ultimately life came—more life than we can possibly imagine. She truly has abundant life—more than we have on this earth. The Word works when we work the Word of God. There is no doubting the restorative power of this incredible eternal healing. No, it was not the way we wanted it, but it does not change our faith or our trust in our Father God. Nor does it change the Word of God. Our faith did not die when Gabrielle's earthly body died.

What more could a daddy ask, but that his daughter be in the loving arms of the worthy Lamb of God for eternity?

He Did It His Way!

The morning of Gabrielle's home-going celebration, Cheryl was in our bathroom getting ready. Posted on the mirror was a petition we had been praying and believing for Gabrielle. Here is what it said:

Petition Granted for Manifestation

1. Tumor dissolved, rooted up and out.
2. Every inch of her body restored—no stretch marks, no broken veins.

3. No facial paralysis.

4. No swelling anywhere, inside or out.

5. Total and complete restoration of eye movement.

6. Total restoration of her smile.

7. Family and finances restored.

As Cheryl pulled this note off the mirror and placed it on the counter, the Holy Ghost spoke to her and said, *I did it!*

Being honest and open about her feelings at that moment she said, "No, You didn't!"

Yes, I did, but I did it My way!

"Well, it wasn't exactly how I wanted You to do it."

But I did it!

Immediately Cheryl was led to this Scripture:

Do not, therefore, fling away your fearless confidence, for it carries a great and glorious compensation of reward. For you have need of steadfast patience and endurance, so that you may perform and fully accomplish the will of God, and thus receive and carry away [and enjoy to the full] what is promised.

HEBREWS 10:35,36 AMP

We speak the Word continually out loud and expect God to perform His Word. That is exactly what He did for Gabrielle—His way, not ours. As long as we are on this earth, we may not understand it, but we completely and totally trust God. We will continue to speak His Word, and God will continue to perform it the same way over and over again because God is not a Man that He should lie!

His Word Works Every Time

This was proven to our family again just three short months later, when Cheryl was diagnosed with colon cancer. We spoke life over her and believed for her healing. I walked with her as she was being wheeled down the hall to surgery. I almost found myself saying to Cheryl, "If you see Jesus with Gabrielle, and you want to go, it's okay with me and the boys. We will be fine." I didn't know what I would do without her, but I wanted her to be happy. I was willing to release her.

Just as we reached the doorway to the surgical suite, as heavily sedated as she already was for surgery, Cheryl opened her eyes, looked at me and said, "I'm not leaving you." That was all I needed to hear. Cheryl had chosen life! I knew in my heart that Cheryl's ultimate desire is to be with Jesus and with Gabrielle, who had gone on ahead. It had to be her choice to remain here on earth.

God has been faithful, and Cheryl has regained her strength. The doctors have given her a good report with each checkup.

As you walk through the turmoil and crises of life, hold on to the promises of God. Don't be afraid to speak His Word. Don't be afraid to step out on a limb, hand Satan the saw and say, "You can saw the limb off or cut the tree down, but this limb is staying right here because I'm standing on the Word of God. I'm standing on His promise, and the Word says..." No matter what evil report comes your way, choose life. Speak God's Word into it, stand on it and believe it. Do what you have to do each day, trusting God and thanking Him for the victory.

Her Body Couldn't Hold Her

by Raven Rubottom

We received this letter from a dear friend who had once worked with me at ORU. It was so encouraging and gave us a new insight into how Gabrielle reached out and received her healing. We felt you would benefit from such truths as only Raven could express them.

—HARRY SALEM

Dear Harry and Cheryl,

We wanted to write and tell you how awesome we thought Gabrielle's memorial service was!

First of all, it was so reflective of your hearts and personality. Giving the WWJD (What Would Jesus Do) wristbands to everybody was so special. Dan wears his all the time. We didn't realize that she was such a little evangelist!

Listening to everybody really gave me the sense that she was of the same spirit as Maria Woodworth Etter, Aimee Semple McPherson and Kathryn Kuhlman. It is no wonder that she was attacked so severely! The enemy knew he had a great contender! My dad said that he knows certain spirits are assigned to harass specific people, but it seemed to him that the devil himself took this one on.

We were so amazed at the hand of God working in that service. With just one day's notice, all the ministers flowed in exactly what God would have them say. They each seemed to deal with the different questions we had about it all—"How do we deal with early death?" "Why?" "What more could we do?" "Does God still heal?" "Is our faith enough?" It was amazing and so resolving.

I must admit that at first I thought Eastman looked like a duck out of water, but he was the one that put a smile back on our faces and began to refocus our attention on the life we were celebrating.

And the other climactic moment was Kenneth Copeland. I must also admit, my eyebrows were raised in wonder as he delicately approached the topic of whether our faith is enough. It was kind of hard to take, but it was absolutely necessary. He has a lot of guts. As my dad commented, "He is true-blue." He didn't have to come to show his support, and he won't get any big accolades, but he did what God said to do, even when it was really hard.

But the most poignant part was when you got up to speak. This was what I needed, and what I think most of the people there needed. It was important to hear that you weren't denying how you felt, that your heart was indeed "broken," but you knew the Healer, and still believed. And that you had done everything you could, the best you could, and had no regrets. It was also so resolving to hear of her final moments on earth. I know it had to be painful to share. It was so intimate and so pure. It is ultimately what has and is resolving the events of this past year in our hearts.

Here I will interject my own personal thoughts based on what you told us. I believe that we can command a body to house the spirit, because that is what God intended it to do. And I believe it was prayer and faith that was holding Gab's little body together. At the same time, it seems that her "spirit man" was so much stronger than her body, it became too much for the weakened vessel to contain any longer. I *don't* believe that she actually made a *choice* between earth and heaven. I believe that when the angels came and the presence of God was so tangible, she actually felt the manifestation of her healing—all the things that Cheryl had listed—and did what anybody would do. She got up off that bed and walked! It's just that her body couldn't keep up with her. It's not that she left Mommy and Daddy behind for something better. I think to her, she was simply accepting her miracle. It was natural for her, because this is what she had believed for—complete freedom from a body that had been holding her captive.

I also believe that she fought so hard and so long, because your love is so strong. And in the end, love never fails.

It was so beautiful to see you both holding each other up, literally, and watch you help each other through talking about the toughest parts—even providing comic relief. You will RE-joice again; the seeds are already growing.

We have always respected you both, and seeing you bond together in marriage and as a family through one difficult ordeal after another has put you at the top of our list. You are just people, we know, we know. But you are what we can only hope to become—so strong, so loving, so faithful. You have *earned* the respect of all who know you, and we love you even more for sharing your most precious memories with us. It was not in vain. We are determined to take what you have taught us over the past months and work harder, go further and instill, ingrain and saturate our children in the Word of God. The Salem family is indeed the model.

Have a rejoicing Christmas and new year!

Dan, Raven, Destiny, Cicely Rubottom

A Royal Child

by Cheryl Salem

Gabrielle Christian Salem was a "Royal Child"—a King's kid—from the moment she was conceived! How do I know that is true? I know it because the fact she was even born was a miracle of God. After hemorrhaging profusely and passing a coffee-cup sized clot early in the pregnancy, the doctor told me I had miscarried this child, but I refused to believe such an evil report. When the bleeding didn't stop, an ultrasound was ordered to determine its cause. The doctor performing the ultrasound confirmed a tumor on my cervix and a couple of tumors on my right ovary. He carefully scanned my entire abdominal area and said, "Well, the baby is fine."

With my own eyes I saw this tiny, little baby kicking and flailing around in my womb on the ultrasound screen.

I had not miscarried. The clot I had passed was actually a fibroid tumor. My baby was alive and living in me! My faith catapulted to a higher level.

Faith Rose Up

The first doctor was not impressed by my excitement or declaration of faith that my baby was alive and kicking. He kept telling me I was bleeding too much, and there was *no hope* for my baby to survive. His evil report fell on deaf ears. I had seen this child, and I knew that I knew that I knew this baby was going to live!

The battle was just beginning, but what Satan meant for evil God used for good. During the next seven months of this pregnancy I was forced to stay flat on my back in bed. Although I was willing to do whatever was necessary to protect my baby, my attitude about being dependent on others to do everything for me and for the boys was far from being loving and submissive. I was used to being in charge of myself and everyone else. Harry said it was like living with King Kong in a cage!

Discover His Unconditional Love

When I finally surrendered my will to the Lord and let Him talk to me instead of me talking to Him, I discovered the beauty of God's unconditional love. He wasn't impressed with my performance-based busyness. He just

wanted me to rest in Him and allow Him to heal some
deep wounds from my childhood. We spent many
wonderful, intimate hours together in the Word and in
prayer. For the first time, I truly basked in His love *for me.*

It's a Girl!

When another ultrasound later in the spring
confirmed this baby was a girl, I was frantic. As a child I
had been sexually abused by someone I dearly loved and
considered to be a "good man." He may have been a good
man, but he had a very bad problem. I kept the abuse a
secret for many years and lived with deep-seated shame
and a sense of unworthiness even for God's love. As a
result, I didn't believe girls could live a "normal life"
because they could never be safe from "good" people.
Being "normal" meant having a safe place to hide from
anyone or anything that could destroy your life. In my
mind, I equated being female with pain and mental and
emotional crippling. I was afraid to have a girl because I
didn't want her to go through the pain I had experienced.

I thought I had dealt with the pain and scars of the
abuse years back, but as God gently pulled off this last
layer of pain and hurt, He began to show me that what I
had gone through had nothing to do with my being a girl.
All the hidden feelings of hurt, anger and distrust of
others began to fade away. God was using this little girl
within my womb to show me the ultimate love the Father

has for His children. He was using this precious angel to show me that His plan goes on regardless of Satan's attacks against us. God was showing me through my baby girl that His abilities are not limited to man or to man's thinking.

God was using this little girl within my womb to show me the ultimate love the Father has for His children.

Satan had lied to me and kept me in fear about having a female child. I finally realized that I had no right to "play God" regarding what the sex of this child I was carrying should be. I had to face the fact that God's will had to be fulfilled through this child, and I had to trust Him with *all* of my children, male or female.

As the weeks of the pregnancy came to a close, I was looking forward to her arrival. I was no longer worried about the outcome of her life. I knew God had His hand upon her, and she would indeed fulfill the call of God on her life. She was after all a "Royal Child."

After a miraculous and *almost* painless delivery, Dr. Mike announced, "It's a girl!" Everyone in the delivery room began to cry because the anointing was so strong! Satan had tried to keep her from being born, but we praised God that she was finally here. She was the most beautiful baby I had ever seen. As I gazed into her eyes,

I felt the healing of the Lord rush all over me. She had brought healing and complete restoration from my past hurts straight from heaven. This was absolute confirmation that God was going to use our little girl for His glory.

As I gazed into her eyes, I felt the healing of the Lord rush all over me.

Gift From Heaven

Harry and I named her Gabrielle Christian Salem, which means "God's Christ-like messenger of peace." She was already fulfilling the prophecy of her name with pure peace over the delivery, over the hospital room and over Harry and me. Here is what I wrote in her baby journal the morning she was born:

> *Dear Precious Little Lady whom God has entrusted into Harry's and my hands—Gabrielle Christian Salem—God's Christ-like messenger of peace—you already have fulfilled the definition of your name through the past months that I have carried you in my tummy…. Now here you are amazing us all, especially me with the healing power of God that you have brought into my life…. Of one thing I am certain: You will carry an even greater anointing than I will ever experience, and God will use you in complete ways that He will only scratch the surface of through my ministry and life.*
>
> *Gabrielle, I love you. I thank you for your strength, your determination, and your willingness to let God use you in*

incredible ways. You are "called," my precious little lady, and the fulfillment of God's promises rest upon your life. You are an extension of what God has started in me, but in a much greater and deeper way.

> *I love you,*
> *Mama*
> *5:30 A.M., May 27, 1993*

Gabrielle did carry a strong anointing upon her even as a baby. When she was only a year old in May 1994, Jessye Ruffin at Covenant Church in Carrollton, Texas, spoke this prophetic word over her:

Thus saith the Lord: I will use this little one to become a fire and a flame to bring an anointing of burning to many nations. My anointing upon her will bring judgment where many will repent and recognize that I am the only true and living God. Revival will ignite internationally because of My fire I will put in her bosom. Her prophetic anointing will bring even conviction to leaders of nations, that My glory may be extended to the ends of the earth. Many as she grows up will misinterpret My fire within her and try to extinguish it, but the Spirit of Truth will always blaze through her—through her eyes and her mouth—for I have anointed her, and, yes, I have called her. Let no one in ignorance extinguish my fire in her bosom!

A Song in Her Heart

A strong love and anointing for music became evident in Gabrielle from an early age. Notes I made in her baby journal when she was only a year old tell how she was trying to sing loudly during praise and worship at church. At seventeen

59

months she would sing to her baby dolls for several minutes, wait for me to sing a little, and then sing some more. By Christmas of that year she was raising her hands and singing with all her might such songs as "Silver Bells," "Jesus Loves Me" and just about anything I would sing.

Her musical gifts developed quickly as she grew, and she was very particular about doing everything right. If the monitor wasn't turned up loud enough for her to hear her music track, she would get upset because she never wanted to sing off-key or lose her place in a song. She made sure her brothers did it right as well!

Persistence and Determination

Gabrielle was the most persistent child you could ever know. When she was about three years old, I was teaching her older brother, Roman, how to receive his prayer language. I told him to cover his eyes so he wouldn't be distracted as he prayed. Gabrielle was listening intently to everything I told him. Later that night I noticed Gabrielle had her hands over her eyes and was saying something over and over. I listened closely, and she was saying, "1, 2, 3, 4, 5, 6, 7, 8, 9" just as fast as she could. It sounded close to a prayer language, and I admired her for her attempt. As determined as Gabrielle was, it was only a couple of days later that I listened again and this time heard her really speaking in tongues! She practiced until she accomplished what she had set out to do. *That* was Gabrielle! She knew what she wanted and went after it until she got it!

From a very early age, Gabrielle knew she was a King's kid. She knew her calling and her purpose in His kingdom, and she never wavered from it. During the year she was sick, she sang and ministered in 100 churches. She laid hands on hundreds of people and prayed for healing, salvation or whatever their needs were.

From a very early age, Gabrielle knew she was a King's kid. She knew her calling and her purpose in His kingdom, and she never wavered from it.

Child of Purpose

The last time she sang at a service was at Rhema Bible Church in June 1999. She hadn't been feeling well that morning. As we gathered in the prayer room prior to the service, Harry said, "Gabrielle, I know you're not feeling well. You don't have to do this." She pointed her finger up in his face with fire in her eyes and said, "Yes, I do. This is what we *do!*" With that, she picked up her IV backpack, went out on the stage and sang, came backstage, threw up and went home. She knew her purpose, and nothing was going to keep her from it.

This was one of Gabrielle's favorite songs, and it truly revealed her heart and her purpose:

Old Enough To Praise the Lord

Too small to be seen in a crowd,
Too young where adults are allowed,
That's why I'm singing out loud,
Cause I'm old enough to praise the Lord.

When I pray, I stand real tall,
In my heart, I can feel His call.
'Cause I know, I'm His precious child,
And I'm old enough to praise the Lord.

It isn't size that makes you wise,
It's what's in your heart that really matters.
When the Son of Man is holding my hand,
That's when I feel a little bigger.

There's a peace that I feel inside,
Cause I know He'll be by my side,
Every day for the rest of my life,
'Cause I'm old enough to praise the Lord.[1]

Gabrielle left her mark on people and on this world. She always wore a WWJD bracelet, and she handed them out to people everywhere she went. She was bold and determined as she walked up to people and said, "Do you know Jesus?" "Let me tell you about My Jesus!" She let her light shine.

A Life Changer!

We received a letter from the daughter of an elderly woman Gabrielle had ministered to at a hospital while she was there for tests. This daughter said, "I know this isn't usually allowed, but I asked the hospital personnel to give me your address off the chart because I had to write and tell you how your little girl impacted my mother's life. My mother is changed and will never be the same." You couldn't stop Gabrielle from shouting out His Word and promises everywhere she went.

After Gabrielle's home-going, a young woman walked up to Harry and said, "I'm called into the music ministry, but I just never had the guts to stand up and sing in front of other people. When I saw your little daughter do it, I was convinced that if such a little girl can do it, then I can do it."

Dr. Oral Roberts once said, "Don't ever go into a meeting without telling them that Gabrielle wasn't just a sweet child. She knew her calling. She sang. She moved people. She laid hands on the sick, and they recovered." What he meant is that Gabrielle was a "Royal Child" and she knew it! She accepted the responsibility that came with it.

Through Her Eyes

When Gabrielle went home to be with Jesus, we didn't know how the prophecies that had been spoken over her were going to be fulfilled, such as the one from Jessye Ruffin and another that said, "Gabrielle won't even have to say a word. When they see her eyes, people will change, nations will change." Since then, Harry and I have been on numerous TV shows, and we always show a video that is a tribute to Gabrielle and share her testimony. We have received letters from people all over the world. One woman said, "When I looked into that little girl's eyes, my life changed."

The prophecies are being fulfilled and her anointing is going forth across the airwaves by television and satellite. Benny Hinn's show and "Praise the Lord" on TBN are broadcast in over 270 nations, not to mention the 700 Club and Oral and Richard Roberts' programs. Recently Salem Family Ministries has received invitations to Ireland and Great Britain. New doors are opening internationally, and Gabrielle goes with us in the Spirit everywhere we go.

The Healed of the Lord

She had a faith beyond her years, and she understood her healing. She spoke the Word and *believed* for her healing. If a man walked into the room and said, "Gabrielle, Jesus is healing you," she would look him in the eye and say, "I AM the healed of the Lord!" If he said, "Your healing is being manifested," immediately she would say, "Jesus *healed* me." If he persisted and said, "Let me pray for your healing," she would say, "Daddy, please ask him to leave the room." This actually happened more than once.

She kept herself built up in the faith by watching her favorite Christian television programs, listening to praise and worship tapes and playing her little keyboard and singing songs to the Lord.

The doctors were amazed at the quality of life Gabrielle had in spite of the diagnosis. The weight gain from the steroids did more to hinder her mobility than the tumor itself. Even when she went into a severe crisis in July while we were in Michigan, she snapped back out of it and was able to color, play her keyboard, sing and give us "attitude."

It wasn't until the last couple of weeks when it got so aggressive that she started losing her body's functions. The last three or four days she couldn't talk, but she could mumble her responses. She knew what we were saying and could squeeze our hands. Her eyes were alert.

The Race was Won!

The doctors gave us two months, but Gabrielle fought the fight and ran the race for eleven months and twelve days. She made a choice on November 23, 1999, to leave the shell she was in, to leave the stretch marks, the stripes on her body, behind. At 7:05 A.M. her little paralyzed face relaxed, her breathing changed from short quick breaths to normal breathing. She began blowing through sweet, puckered lips like she was kissing the angels around her as she left with her heavenly escort.

Gabrielle Christian Salem was and is a "Royal Child"— a King's kid. She touched and changed more people for the kingdom of God in

Gabrielle Christian Salem was and is a "Royal Child"–a King's kid. She touched and changed more people for the kingdom of God in her short six years on this earth than most people do in an adult lifetime.

her short six years on this earth than most people do in an adult lifetime. She had an anointing for healing that began in the womb, as my own life was healed, and is still reaching around the globe today. Her destiny is being fulfilled as her testimony goes forth in this book and as Salem Family Ministries spreads the gospel to the nations of the world.

Satan uses crises as entry points to fill your mind with lies that produce doubt and fear to rob you of your hope and to steal your most prized possessions. Don't let him get away with it. Stand up to him and remind him that you are a King's kid and he can't touch you because you are covered in the blood of Jesus. You have the authority to stop him in his tracks. You *are* a "Royal Child" with a purpose in God's kingdom. Embrace your calling and purpose, as Gabrielle did hers, and don't let anything stop you from fulfilling your destiny. If a little six-year-old girl can do it, so can you!

Satan uses crises as entry points to fill your mind with lies that produce doubt and fear to rob you of your hope and to steal your most prized possessions. Don't let him get away with it.

With Love, Nanny

by Tracey Jacobs

I got you a Barbie card on your seventh birthday. I remember when we went to the grocery store right before you turned six, and you picked out and bought the cards that you wanted everyone to give you. You sure did make everyone smile with that one! That's what you always did— you made everyone feel better. Seeing your beautiful face always made whatever problems or situations of the day seem so insignificant. Your smile always erased the shadows.

But you know, what you did with the birthday cards, that's just like you. I mean, you always knew exactly what you were doing and you always knew just what to say. Like Daddy says, "Gabrielle knew her purpose." You always did. Oh, how I want to be more like you! Through it all—from January 11, 1999 to the end of November—you never complained. You never asked "Why?" You handled everything that came at you with so much grace! I am so, so very proud of you.

I remember coming to the airport to pick all of you up after a ministry trip. I would wait with the other folks who were there to pick up their friends and family, and I would think to myself, *Wait till they see who I'm picking up!* You would come down that jet way from the plane into the airport, and my heart would jump when I'd see you! Usually, I'd hear you long before I'd get to see you! Other passengers who had been on the same plane always looked over at you and smiled as they made their way to wherever they were going—smiling over at you because you had stolen their hearts on the flight. But then there you would be, with your little rolling suitcase, your purse, a Barbie or a baby doll tucked under your arm and a huge smile, hug and kiss for me. There was that one time in particular that you were arriving from L.A. and you came off the plane with your white ruffled shirt, new black bell-bottom pants, black clog shoes and blue-tinted round sunglasses! So cool! I thought I couldn't possibly ever smile any bigger than I did when I saw you right then.

Thinking of you now, though, I always do smile. I think of you making cakes and decorating them with *everything* in the kitchen; riding your bike around the kitchen singing, "Something Good Tonight," with Barbies, chocolate milk and baby dolls in the basket of your bike; cruising in your pink Barbie car; primping in the mirror; painting everyone's fingernails, toenails and even my legs with that blue paint; racing up and down the driveway with Roman for hours at a time; begging to go swimming when it was too cold outside (and usually getting to try it!); climbing all over Harry like he was a jungle gym (and him just letting you do it!); calling me from Mommy and Daddy's cell phone to tell me that there were donuts for you on the plane (you were so excited!). I remember you coming down the stairs in the morning, dressed and ready for school and having done it all by yourself! You could always handle anything.

Mommy and I were watching you from the window the day you jumped into the deep end of the pool. We knew you could swim, because you would swim like a fish all around the shallow end. Meagan and Amanda were there, jumping and playing in the deep end. Well, while Mommy and I watched and held our breath, you pondered for a minute, set your mind to it, stepped back, took a running start and leaped into the deep end. From then on, you swam anywhere and everywhere you wanted to swim.

You met challenges, dealt with them and overcame them. I have never known anyone like you. You have changed me and made me better. Every single day, I want so desperately to see you, to hear your precious voice coming from your room singing (usually your favorite—*Hillsongs* praise and worship music) as you happily play Barbies for hours, and to have you run and jump into my lap to watch *Parent Trap* with me. But, as Mommy says all the time, "We've got to become more heavenly-minded than earthly-minded." She's right. When I think of heaven and of all the incredible things you are seeing and doing right now—when I think of how you are with Jesus—I can't possibly remain so selfish.

I thank God with my whole heart that He allowed me to be a part of your life. You have changed my life forever. I love you.

Wahoo! God Is Able!

by Harry Salem

Nothing is impossible when you tap into the *real* power source—the power that Jesus has to save you, heal you and set you free! No matter how tough the battle is, you can walk in victory if you stay focused on the power source of the Anointed One, Jesus Christ. Here are two important keys to remember when you are in spiritual warfare:

1. *Focus* on your miracle not on the circumstances, no matter how devastating they appear to be.
2. *Don't limit God*, because you might miss the greatest gift He has for you.

Kicked Back but Not Down

When we listened to the devastating, evil report from the doctors about Gabrielle, we were initially in shock. It was like being kicked back, but not down, by a mule and having the wind knocked out of us; but we quickly came to our senses. This was the toughest battle we had ever faced, but we knew what we had to do: look to *the Healer.* We could not look to the doctors, because there was no earthly cure. I have always said, "Don't go to the repairman; go to the Manufacturer, God!" The

"Don't go to the repairman; go to the Manufacturer, God!"

doctors gave us no hope, but we have a covenant relationship with the Great Physician, and it was in Him we placed our hope. Immediately we *focused* on the miracle of Gabrielle's healing. We set our faces like flint (Isa. 50:7.) and never looked back, because we know from whom we receive our power.

Focus on the Healer

This wasn't the first life-and-death battle we had faced, and we were prepared to fight. We would not give up, and we would not give ground to the enemy. Day by day for over eleven months we dealt with what was happening in the natural to our precious little girl's body, but we kept our focus on her healing, not on the circumstances. We looked to Jesus—the very source, the author of life.

The Scriptures are filled with reports of miracles performed by Jesus and later by His disciples. We can learn a great deal from these accounts about appropriating a miracle. Let's look at one told in the book of Acts about a crippled man who was healed at the gate of the temple in Jerusalem.

> *Now Peter and John were going up to the temple at the hour of prayer, the ninth hour (three o'clock in the afternoon).*
>
> ACTS 3:1 AMP

Notice here that Peter and John had an appointed time to pray each day. They had a relationship with God and talked with Him regularly. The first step to appropriating a miracle is to pray and have a relationship with the Father so you can recognize His voice and take direction from Him. Let's read on further in this passage.

The first step to appropriating a miracle is to pray and have a relationship with the Father so you can recognize His voice and take direction from Him.

> *[When] a certain man crippled from birth was being carried along, who was laid each day at that gate of the temple [which is] called Beautiful, so that he might beg for charitable gifts from those who entered the temple. So when he saw Peter and John about to go into the temple, he asked them to give him a gift.*
>
> ACTS 3:2,3 AMP

Don't Limit God

It is important to note this man asked for a gift. He probably didn't know Peter and John, but begging was the only way he had to get his needs met. He didn't say, "Give me money," or "Give me a car." Even though he expected to receive some sort of financial assistance, he didn't limit God. He simply said, "Give me a gift." And boy, did God have a gift for him! Another step to appropriating a miracle is not putting limitations on what we ask God to do. When we don't limit God, He will give us far above and beyond what we ask or think.

We have ministered in Los Angeles many times and have driven along the downtown streets, where many homeless people live. We wanted our children to understand how people live in many different walks of life, so we pointed out the homeless people, many of whom had all their earthly possessions stuffed into old shopping carts. For months after one of these trips, whenever Gabrielle saw people with shopping carts in the grocery store, she would say, "Are they homeless?" We had to tell her, "No, they aren't homeless. They are just doing their grocery shopping."

Look Up!

It really wasn't the shopping cart that set these homeless people apart. Many of them were begging, as distinguished by the beggar's position they assumed—head down, hand out! Have you ever seen a man begging? He won't look you in the eye. He just sticks his hand out expecting you to hand him some money. This man in the Bible was no different; but Peter and John knew that if this man was going to get out of the situation he was in and change his life forever, he had to learn to focus on something different than what he had been focusing on all of his life. That is why they said to him, "Look at us!"

> *And Peter directed his gaze intently at him, and so did John, and said, Look at us! And [the man] paid attention to them, expecting that he was going to get something from them.*
>
> ACTS 3:4,5 AMP

They wanted him to focus on what they had to give him: life! Let's read further:

> *But Peter said, Silver and gold (money) I do not have; but what I do have, that I give to you: in [the use of] the name of Jesus Christ of Nazareth, walk!*
>
> *Then he took hold of the man's right hand with a firm grip and raised him up. And at once his feet and ankle bones became strong and steady, and leaping forth he stood and began to walk, and he went into the temple with them, walking and leaping and praising God.*
>
> ACTS 3:6-8 AMP

Peter and John wanted this man to know they had something more than a little money to get him through to the next day. They had something that was going to change his life forever—Jesus. They spoke with authority; and when he looked at them, he paid attention and believed them.

The Power of Covenant Agreement

It took both the supernatural power of the name of Jesus *and* the natural strength of Peter reaching down and lifting this man up onto his feet for this man's miracle to manifest. When Peter took this man's hand in his, they came into covenant agreement and power went forth. When Peter said, "In the name of Jesus Christ of Nazareth, walk!" the man believed and was healed. This man had to look beyond his circumstances and focus on what Peter and John said to him. He had to look beyond what he was used to doing every day.

Ask and Believe!

If you want your miracle, you have to pray and specifically ask the Father for it. You can't just shoot with a shotgun in the spirit realm and expect to hit anything. You have to stay focused on your miracle with expectation until you get it. Don't give up just because it doesn't come

You can't just shoot with a shotgun in the spirit realm and expect to hit anything.

when or how you expect. That is putting a limit on God, and you may miss out on the greatest gift God has for you that goes far beyond that for which you are believing.

The man in this Scripture was begging for alms, and God gave him new legs. He went walking and leaping into the temple, praising God. God always does superabundantly, far above and beyond that which we dare ask.

Plug in to the Power Source

I was once with ORU president, Richard Roberts, in a crusade in Nigeria and saw a similar healing take place. Abdul was a crippled man who begged on the street corner. Everyone knew him. Like the man in the Scripture we read, he had no one carrying him around. The only way Abdul could get around was by taking aluminum Coca Cola cans in his hands so he wouldn't bloody his knuckles as he scraped himself along the ground. Abdul came to the crusade grounds one night, and I saw him scuffle in. People made a way for him so he could get close enough to see the platform.

When President Roberts began to pray for the sick, some people brought Abdul up on the stage. President Roberts reached down to him and said, "I'm going to grab you with power and get you up on your feet." There was that covenant power of agreement again. Abdul was healed and started leaping and jumping. The crowd went wild and the more they clapped the more he jumped.

All of a sudden, Abdul squatted back down on the floor. Through an interpreter, President Roberts said, "Why did you go back down? You were healed. Get up and walk!" The problem was Abdul had never been up so high and he was scared. The crowd kept clapping, and Abdul got back up on his feet. The more they clapped the more he gained strength in his legs and walked back and forth. Abdul had plugged in to the power source, just as the crippled man did in the book of Acts. For Abdul, the clapping was the spark to ignite the ammunition for the power to go forth.

The word *clap* in Hebrew means, "to strike the hands together in praise, to strike the hands together in victory, to have a surety or a guarantee of the promise, an absolute, covenant relationship or guaranteed assurance." Isn't that awesome?

Clap Your Way to Victory

Clapping is actually a form of spiritual warfare. When you clap your hands together, it is a sign of a guarantee that you believe, receive and walk in the promise God has given you for your miracle. You are clapping your hands together in agreement with God that the promise is given, received and fulfilled in Jesus' mighty name. Whether it is healing, provision of finances, restoration of your marriage or bringing a wayward child home, it is already a done deal.

The devil doesn't want to turn you or your loved one loose or submit to your power, but he doesn't have any choice, as it says in this Scripture:

> *Through the greatness of Your power shall Your enemies submit themselves to You [with feigned and reluctant obedience].*

> PSALM 66:3 AMP

The word *power* in the Greek means, "the strength of God bestowed upon believers." It means "might, the ability to perform, to work and to carry things into effect." There is a fine line that stands between "I believe I receive" and "there it is." It takes the power of God to take a miracle from "I believe I receive" to "there it is," carrying it into effect from the supernatural into the natural.

It takes the power of God to take a miracle from "I believe I receive" to "there it is," carrying it into effect from the supernatural into the natural.

Today Is Victory!

No matter why, by whom or how we were being attacked, we knew we had to look up and stay focused on Gabrielle's healing. In the face of the daily battles we were facing, this wasn't easy; but then the Lord spoke a word to me that gave us a tremendous breakthrough. He said, *I will allow you two thoughts. You can think about today and do what you have to do today and, having done all the crisis demands, stand. The other thought you can have is victory. Think of nothing in between. Don't think about anything but today and victory. As far as you're concerned, today is victory!*

Those two thoughts bring the starting line and the finish line together. You start and that's today. You do what you have to do to get through the crisis today. You never allow yourself to think, *What about tomorrow? What about birthdays?* You think about victory today because that is what you have—today and victory—nothing else. When those two become one, you're settled.

Limiting yourself to those two thoughts pulls your thought life into submission. Every time a different thought comes at you and tries to make you think about the "what ifs" and the "yes, buts," you just say, "In the name of Jesus, I do not allow that thought into my mind." You can't fight a thought with another thought. You fight thoughts with words from the Word of God. To live in victory, you must pull down every vain imagination and take every fleeting thought captive, as it says in this Scripture:

You can't fight a thought with another thought. You fight thoughts with words from the Word of God.

> *(For the weapons of our warfare are not carnal, but mighty through God to the pulling down of strong holds;) casting down imaginations, and every high thing that exalteth itself against the knowledge of God, and bringing into captivity every thought to the obedience of Christ.*
>
> 2 CORINTHIANS 10:4,5

The devil takes every opportunity to try to defeat us with thoughts in our minds. That is where the battle rages.

When you are in the midst of a battle, you have to rebuke the devourer—the devil—every single day. We learned this in the early days of our battle.

Keep On Keeping On

It was Super Bowl Sunday in January 1999. We had been at the clinic in Houston with Gabrielle for only a week or so and were released to preach at a church not far from Houston. We were running late, and about a half a mile from the church we ran out of fuel with the motor coach. It's illogical to run out of fuel in a vehicle that has a 120-gallon fuel tank, but it happened. To say I was distraught was an understatement. I grabbed the cellular phone and called AAA®.

"Ma'am."

"Yes."

"We're here in Cleveland, Texas, and we've run out of fuel. I need you to send somebody."

"You're in Cleveland, Ohio?"

"No, ma'am, I'm in Cleveland, *Texas.*"

"Cleveland, Tennessee?"

"No, ma'am, I'm in Cleveland, *Texas!*"

"Now, where are you?"

"What do you mean? I just told you."

"Well, I got that, but what street are you on?"

I had to get out of the motor coach and walk down the street to find a street sign. All of a sudden the phone went dead. I had walked out of the range of the cellular tower. I redialed AAA, and the conversation started all over again with a different customer service representative.

"No, I'm not in Cleveland, Tennessee. I'm in Cleveland, *Texas.*"

"Well, where are you?"

I told him the name of the road.

"Well, where are you on the road?"

"I'm smack-dab in the middle of the road!"

"Well, can you push it out of the road?"

"A thirty-five-foot motor coach? I don't think so…"

I was so upset by that time that I hung up and called the church. Someone brought a can of diesel fuel, but we still couldn't get it started. When you have a 120-gallon fuel tank and you only put five gallons of diesel fuel in it, it's like spitting on a fire. We had to leave the motor coach there and ride to the church with someone else.

Sitting on the platform, I was not focused on the service. My conversation with the Lord went something like this: "It's Super Bowl Sunday, and no one is going to be working. Without the motor coach we aren't going to be able to get back to the clinic. The whole thing is just going down the tubes. Lord, this is just too hard. I can't do it!"

The Lord said, *Harry, you keep doing what you're called to do, and I'll do what I am called to do.*

That was a "rhema," life-giving word from the Lord, and it set me free.

Later I said to Cheryl, "Cheryl, we've got to keep doing this. We've got to keep ministering. God will keep rebuking the devourer." From that day forward we stood on the promise of God's Word, as it says here:

> *"And I will rebuke the devourer for your sakes, so that he will not destroy the fruit of your ground, nor shall the vine fail to bear fruit for you in the field," says the Lord of hosts.*

MALACHI 3:11 NKJV

Find Your Voice of Triumph

On the first Saturday night after we received the doctor's report about Gabrielle, the phone rang at two o'clock in the morning. I answered and it was my sister, Lindsay Roberts.

Barely conscious I said, "Don't you ever go to sleep at a proper hour?"

"We never do. I've got a word for you. The Lord told me to tell you 'Wahoo!'"

"You're interrupting my sleep at two in the morning to tell me 'Wahoo?'"

At this point I handed the phone to Cheryl and let Lindsay explain this strange word from the Lord to her.

Lindsay said, "The Lord reminded me of that movie, *IQ*. In the movie, Albert Einstein befriended a little mechanic who owned a motorcycle. Einstein loved riding on the motorcycle. Every time the mechanic took Einstein for a ride and they went over a hill, his back end would come up off the seat, and he would yell, 'Wahoo!' With every hill or bump in the road, he yelled, 'Wahoo!' The Lord said, *Tell Harry and Cheryl it's Wahoo time!*"

Naturally, Cheryl caught the excitement of it and said, "Harry, it's Wahoo time! That's what they're saying."

"You're all nuts!"

"Harry, talk to them. I've got to write it on all the mirrors." She ran to get her red lipstick and wrote "Wahoo!" on all the mirrors in the house.

Not wanting to get in the middle of some "girl" thing, I said, "Let me talk to Richard." As I picked up the phone, I could hear Richard in the background yelling, "Wahoo! Wahoo!" like he was riding a bucking bronco or a wild stallion. Richard—an educated man, a down-to-earth kind of guy and the president of Oral Roberts University—was yelling "Wahoo!" but I still didn't get it.

By this time Cheryl was jumping on the bed yelling, "Wahoo! Wahoo! Wahoo!" Then she said, "Harry, go wake your mom up and tell her 'Wahoo!'"

"Not me. I'm not going in there at two o'clock in the morning. I still remember when she stood on a chair and said, 'I can still whip you, boy.'"

"You get in there and tell your mother, 'Wahoo!'"

"Okay."

I went and knocked on the door to her room. One of the boys opened the door, and I said, "Mama." There was silence. A little louder I said, "Mama."

"Yes."

"Wahoo!"

"What, honey?"

"Wahoo!"

"That's nice..."

"Lindsay said to tell you, 'Wahoo!'"

"Well, if Lindsay said it, 'Wahoo!'" With that, she went back to sleep.

This may sound as crazy to you as it did to me that night, but it was the following Scripture we found in Isaiah that explained this word from the Lord:

> *But this is a people robbed and plundered; all of them are snared in holes, and they are hidden in prison houses; they are for prey, and no one delivers; for plunder, and no one says, "Restore!"*

ISAIAH 42:22 NKJV

God was really upset with His people because He had given them all the weapons they needed for warfare, and they hadn't done anything with them. They just let the enemy beat the tar out of them. God's people were robbed, plundered and destroyed because no one would jump up and shout, "Restore!"

My five-year-old daughter led me to my voice of triumph, and "Wahoo!" became our battle cry.

Cheryl read this and said, "Harry, the enemy is trying to rob, plunder and steal from us, and it is time to shout, 'Wahoo!' because God is able!" (She had looked up the Hebrew word *yahu* and it means,

"God is able.") "With every bump in the road, we need to shout, 'Wahoo!'"

I didn't yell, "Wahoo" right then, but I pondered that Scripture.

The doctor told us Gabrielle needed to get more exercise, so we took her to a city park. The boys and I took her up and down a big thirty-two-foot slide, and she was laughing. Next she wanted to go on the swing set, and as I was pushing her, Gabrielle was saying, "Wahoo!" "Wahoo!" I finally got it! "Wahoo!" "Wahoo!" "Wahoo!" began to just come out of my mouth. My five-year-old daughter led me to my voice of triumph, and "Wahoo!" became our battle cry.

Are you tired of being robbed and stolen from? Are you tired of being hidden in a cave and snared in a hole? Then, jump up and shout "Wahoo!" You may not know where (in my case, it was in a park) or when (in the midst of tragedy) or by whom (a little girl) you will find your voice of triumph. Between "I believe I receive" and "there it is" comes "Wahoo! God is able!" Shout "Wahoo!" and clap your hands as a surety, a

Shout "Wahoo!" and clap your hands as a surety, a guarantee that your miracle is a done deal.

guarantee that your miracle is a done deal. This is spiritual warfare for your family, for your home, for your finances and your health. We stand with you in covenant agreement as you tap into the real power source in the mighty name of Jesus and shout, "Wahoo! God *is* able!"

What Are You Doing With What You Have?

by Eastman Curtis

When I think of Gabrielle and her life here on earth, Jude 1:22 readily comes to mind: "On some have compassion making a difference." That word compassion is used nine times in the Gospel accounts in the New Testament. Every time you see the Bible recording that Jesus had compassion—whether it was on the multitude or on an individual—look out, because a miracle is about to happen. There is something very powerful about having compassion, about taking your eyes off yourself and looking at the needs of the people around you. And I can tell you, that is exactly what Gabrielle did.

It's not what you have so much as what you *do* with what you have that makes the difference. Gabrielle only had six years to make a difference in this world, and look at what she did with those few short years. She affected the world with her smile, her vitality for life and her love for people.

The day before Gabrielle's celebration service, Richard and Lindsay Roberts, Harry and I were sitting at the table talking about some of the things that Gabrielle did. Whenever Gabrielle found out that Aunt Lindsay was coming over, she would go sit in the driveway with her great big Super Soaker. She knew she could make a difference with that Super Soaker. When Lindsay got out of the car, she was instantly "baptized" by it. According to Richard, Lindsay would have to change clothes three or four times during the course of her visit.

Richard also told me how Gabrielle would occasionally come in with a baseball bat, convinced that one of her brothers needed to be "whooped." And she would take it upon herself to do the "whooping." As soon as her brothers started to cry, she'd run in the other room, hold up her hands and say, "That's okay. I repent. It's all right. It's going to be okay. I repent." The good thing about Gabrielle was that she was quick to repent. A few minutes later, she would do it all over again—loving life, but still making a difference.

The one thing she could not stand was to be told she could not do something because she was too young or that it was impossible for her. She knew she could do *all* things through Christ who strengthened her. (Phil. 4:13.) This confidence in her ability to accomplish anything in Christ was something that filled every aspect of her life. One day her brothers were doing the WWF thing, wrestling on the carpet. Little Harry looked up and said, "Girls can't wrestle." Then Roman confidently chimed in and said, "I *know* girls can't wrestle." Well that's all it took for little

Gabrielle. She reached over, lifted up the ottoman made of steel and leather and promptly squished her brothers with it. Putting her hands on her hips, she smiled and said, "I told you, girls *can* wrestle."

It's not what you have; it's what you *do* with what you have that makes the difference. On some, having compassion is the way to make a difference. Even with all that she was going through herself, Gabrielle took her eyes off herself and looked at the needs of the people around her. She never complained one time. Harry said, "Never once did I ever hear her complain. Never once did I hear her say, 'I'm sick. I feel terrible.' She never said that. Instead of focusing on her own problems, she looked at the needs of the people around her."

Gabrielle was always concerned about ministering to other people. She carried her little IV pack (it weighed 25 percent of her total body weight) around on her shoulder while she ministered. It was so heavy it caused her shoulder to hang down from the weight, but that didn't stop her. She carried it through prayer lines while laying hands on people, letting the healing anointing of God flow through her.

Her ministry crossed denominational barriers. I even heard that there were monks in Scandinavia praying for this little girl with great faith. Again, it's not what you have; it's what you *do* with what you have.

Now is not the time to back off. Now is the time to press in with our faith like never before. Now is the time to stand up and be the men and women of God that He has called us to be. What are we going to do with what God has given us? On some, we need to have compassion and make a difference that way. I want my life to make a difference, and I know that God wants you to make a difference with what He has given you.

What other six-year-old girl has had two record albums produced, ministered 265 times in one year and (up to three weeks before she died) still traveled with her family while fighting the last stages of cancer. When I look at little Gabrielle's life, it makes me want to run harder and preach more. I want to unload hell and load up heaven with the Good News of what God has done. It's not what we have; it's what we *do* with what we have that is going to make a difference. Her love for life, along with her tenacious faith and her passion for people, did just that. God wants us to follow her example and let it impact lives for years to come. I want to let it motivate me to run harder.

Whenever Gabrielle went to the clinic or to a hospital for tests, she carried a handful of little WWJD bracelets with her. She did something with those little bracelets to make a difference in the lives of the people there. She handed them out to people and brightened their day. Just take a moment to think about the message of the bracelets she handed out. "What would Jesus do?" I'll tell you what He would do. He would take His eyes off Himself and look at the needs of people around Him, just as Gabrielle did.

Here is a story from the Gospels that radically changed my life. Matthew 14:13 tells us that when Jesus found out that His best friend, John the Baptist, had been beheaded, He got into a boat to go to a solitary place to be alone for awhile. But the crowd heard that the "Miracle Man," Jesus, had gone to the other side of the lake. When Jesus arrived at the other side and stepped out of the boat, He saw a huge crowd standing by the lake. The smell of sickness and disease was in the air. Next a demon-possessed lunatic came up to Him, and the people started screaming, "Jesus, heal me! Jesus, heal me!"

In the natural, most of us would look out at those people and think, *Don't you understand? My best friend just died.* What did Jesus do? He took His eyes off Himself and looked at the needs of the people around Him. The Bible says He **was moved with compassion toward them, and he healed their sick.** (v. 14.)

I want you to know something. It's a fact that Jesus came 2000 years ago. It's a fact that He walked on the earth. It's a fact that He healed the sick, cleansed the lepers, cast out devils and raised the dead. It's a fact that He died on the cross of Calvary for our sins, for our sicknesses and for our poverty. It's a fact that they put His body in a tomb; and it's a fact that on the third day, the stone was rolled away, and Jesus Christ walked out alive. It's a fact that He ascended into heaven. It's a fact that He's coming again. And it is a fact that right now Gabrielle is in heaven rejoicing. It's not what you have; it's what you *do* with what you have that makes a difference. What are you doing with what you have?

Plant Seeds for the Harvest

by Harry Salem

Anyone who has ever done any gardening knows you have to plant seeds in order to reap a harvest. This principle of sowing and reaping is true in nature *and* in the spiritual realm. It is also a fact that a seed produces after its own kind, so what you plant is what you will harvest. You can't plant corn and expect to harvest potatoes, nor can you plant seeds of anger and expect to receive love or peace in return. This holds true in every aspect of life.

A Seed of Transportation

With the thousands of miles we are traveling each year from one end of the country to the other, we need faster, more efficient transportation. We need an airplane. The

Lord recently impressed upon us to sow our van into another ministry. It had a few miles on it, but it was in very good condition. A van isn't an airplane, but it is transportation. We realized God wanted us to plant a transportation seed for our airplane. We gave it to a church with a great youth ministry in another state where there was a serious need. Since that time, the funds have been pouring in for our airplane.

Plant for a Future Harvest

A garden doesn't grow overnight. Once it is planted, it has to be watered and cultivated for a period of time before the plants peek up out of the ground and then grow to maturity. The same is true in the spiritual realm. We must get a good quality and quantity of seed in the ground so that it will be ready to harvest when we need it. It is like putting money in a savings account so that when a rainy day comes you have the funds necessary to get through the storm. In every area of life,

It is absolutely essential to get the Word in you before the crisis so when you get squeezed, the Word comes out.

you have to make deposits before you can make withdrawals. It is absolutely essential to get the Word in you *before* the crisis so when you get squeezed, the Word comes out.

Cheryl and I have embraced these principles and taught our children the importance of planting seed for a future harvest. We have planted the Word of God in them from the time of conception and demonstrated for them how important it is to give out of their hearts to others. Our family is living proof that when you do this, the harvest will be there when you need it.

Expect a Harvest

Because Gabrielle's medical treatment regime at the clinic in Houston was considered alternative medicine, insurance would not pay the costs. When I first learned what the cost was going to be—approximately $24,000 up front and then $15,000 per month—I was talking with Richard Roberts and said, "Richard, my God is not going to make me sell pencils on the street corner to pay for this. We have planted good seed in His kingdom, and we *expect* a harvest."

The first check we wrote to the clinic was for $30,000. Cheryl and I paid that out of our own pockets because we wanted to sow into Gabrielle's healing. That just covered the first month's clinic visit and expenses. We were looking at the possibility of two years or more for a complete regimen of treatments.

In the natural all these expenses looked devastatingly impossible, but immediately as the needs arose the harvest began to come in. The hotel bill during that first month at the clinic was nearly $5000. Since we were going to be at the clinic for so long, we knew we needed a kitchen and space for all seven of us. Tracey and my mom were with us to help with the boys. The Marriott Corporation was unable to place us in the two rooms with a kitchen that we needed, so they located two rooms in another hotel and paid for one of the rooms. When we were ready to check out, I went to the front desk to pay the bill and handed the desk clerk our credit card. She said, "Your bill is already paid in full."

I thought she was mistaken and said, "No, Marriott blessed us and paid for one room, but we owe you for the balance."

She responded, "No sir, a person called this morning and said, "This is my credit card number, and I want to pay the Salem's hotel bill. However, I don't want them to know who is paying it."

To this day we don't know who paid that bill, but that was the beginning of our harvest coming in. Every month the bills for the clinic, prescriptions, laboratory work, supplies, travel, and so forth, accumulated; and every month checks came in from people all over the country to pay off the bills. One day we had taken the children to a Chuck E. Cheese® restaurant, and a wonderful couple from Dallas, who came just to be with us, handed me a $5000 check. Checks continued to arrive in the mail for $10, $20,

$100, $500, and $1000. One lady sent us seven cents because she wanted to help and that was all she had. When we had to stop the medical treatments with the clinic in Houston and our expenses dropped, so did the amount of money coming in. Later, when there was a greater need once again, it increased. God knew exactly what we needed, and His provision was sufficient. The sum of about $200,000 in medical bills and expenses was paid in full! Miraculously, some medical treatments and lab work were donated by a few facilities.

Seeds Are More Than Money

Not only did people send money, but they also sent words of encouragement, books and teaching tapes they thought would be helpful. We listened to teaching tapes and played praise music constantly to keep ourselves built up in the Spirit. We kept the Word fresh in our hearts and minds and spoke it out of our mouths. Here is one Scripture that was a standard for us:

No weapon formed against you shall prosper…

ISAIAH 54:17 NKJV

The Hebrew word for prosper is *solak,* which means "break through to success." In other words, any weapon the enemy uses against you cannot break through to success. No weapon formed against you will break through God's shield and armor.

95

Be of Good Cheer

In this Scripture, Jesus told us we would have trouble; and then he added a key phrase:

"These things I have spoken to you, that in Me you may have peace. In the world you will have tribulation; but be of good cheer, I have overcome the world."

JOHN 16:33 NKJV

We should never let go of the "but" phrases like this one—*but* **be of good cheer.** No matter what trouble we are going through, Jesus has already overcome it. Be of good cheer, for you have weapons to stop the devil in his tracks and destroy his works. When you clap your hands in praise, that is a weapon. When you pray in the morning, that is a weapon. When you take another believer's hand and stand in agreement, that is a weapon. When you put on your armor each morning, that is a weapon.

Be of good cheer, for you have weapons to stop the devil in his tracks and destroy his works.

Don't Forget Your Armor

We have taught our children to put on their godly armor every single morning. We must not be ignorant of the devil's ways, and it is pure ignorance not to use the weapons God has given us. In biblical days fiery darts were lethal weapons. The shaft of an arrow was hollow. Warriors filled the shaft with a combustible fluid and then placed a tip on the end that would cause it to strike like a flint when it hit something hard. When such an arrow was fired into the chest of someone and hit the bone, it would explode into fire.

The devil's fiery darts are just as lethal, but we have the shield of faith to deflect the arrow and the water of the Word to quench the fire. Let me explain something about shields used in biblical days. The Romans were trained for battle, and a shield was made from leather hides stretched around a frame to make it tough and impenetrable. The soldiers rubbed oil on their shields to keep them pliable, so that when the fiery arrows struck the shield, they would bounce off. Then before

You can't fight the devil with your fists. You have to fight him with the Word of God and in the power of His Spirit.

battle they soaked their shields in water. That way if an arrow happened to stick in the shield, the water extinguished the flame.

Likewise, when you soak in the oil of the anointing of the Holy Spirit, your shield of faith deflects the devil's fiery darts. You do this by praying in the Spirit every day to keep yourself pliable, flexible and adaptable to what God is doing. You also need to soak in the water of the Word of God to be able to put out the fire. When you don't pray in the Spirit, you get hardened to the things of God; and without a washing of the Word, you have nothing to put out the fire to keep the enemy's lies and deceptions from exploding inside of you. You can't fight the devil with your fists. You have to fight him with the Word of God and in the power of His Spirit.

Use Weapons as Seeds

Think of these weapons—the oil of the Spirit and the water of the Word—as seeds you plant each day. As you keep planting and planting, when the crisis comes, you will be able to stand firmly in your place.

There is another weapon we can read about in this Scripture:

> *Bring all the tithes (the whole tenth of your income) into the storehouse, that there may be food in My house, and prove Me now by it, says the Lord of hosts, if I will not open the windows of heaven for you and pour you out a blessing, that there shall not be room enough to receive it. And I will rebuke the devourer [insects and plagues] for your sakes and he shall not destroy the fruits of your ground, neither shall your vine drop its fruit before the time in the field, says the Lord of hosts.*

> MALACHI 3:10,11 AMP

Your tithe is a weapon, and God says He will rebuke the devourer—the seedeater. Did you know that of the Christians who say they attend church regularly, only 12 percent of them tithe? Does that give you any clue as to why the body of Christ is under such attack? Yes, the devil is a bad devil, and he has the ability to form weapons against you, but God is ready and willing to rebuke the devourer. He is chomping at the bit to bless His people, but He can't because they aren't following the rules and staying in covenant relationship with Him. They are disobedient to His Word regarding paying tithes, and then they get mad at Him when things go wrong.

God won't go against His Word. He says, "If you follow My laws, I'm giving you a guarantee that you will be blessed beyond what you can imagine. I'm giving you a tool: your money!"

Let Faith Arise

We were not only attacked by the evil report from the devil, but then he tried to attack our finances by telling us, "Your insurance won't cover it." That is when our faith had to rise up. I said, "Cheryl, we have to *believe* we can do it and go to the clinic. We are going to pay for it somehow, but it's going to have to be God."

We went to this Scripture in Malachi and stood on the truth that for years we had tithed over 10 percent of our income from our company, our ministry and our personal incomes. Then we looked at what we had given in offerings. An offering is something that has no predetermined return. That means you can expect an unlimited return. We gave away 20,000 children's books in 1998 alone. We sowed into the lives of many other pastors, churches, ministries and individuals with our finances and with our love.

We said, "Now, Lord, we've done what You told us to do. We're taking that other tool, our tithe, off the shelf right now and standing on it because You said You are going to rebuke the devourer, the seedeater. We have a guarantee, a surety and an agreement with You, and we know You will do Your part." We had put good seed in the ground, and now we were claiming our harvest in this time of crisis.

We also picked up another tool spoken of in Scripture:

Inasmuch then as we have a great High Priest Who has [already] ascended and passed through the heavens, Jesus the Son of God, let us hold fast our confession [of faith in Him].

Let us then fearlessly and confidently and boldly draw near to the throne of grace (the throne of God's unmerited favor to us sinners), that we may receive mercy [for our failures] and find grace to help in good time for every need [appropriate help and well-timed help, coming just when we need it].

HEBREWS 4:14,16 AMP

That tool was *holding fast to the confession of our faith.* Many people quote this Scripture for salvation, but it is meant for more than that. We held on to the confession of our faith for Gabrielle's restoration and for everything we would need to walk through the fire during this crisis and beyond. His Word says that by His grace we will find the help we need, exactly when we need it.

Boldly Confess Your Faith

What is your confession for healing? Are you boldly confessing, "By the stripes that wounded Jesus, I am healed and completely made whole"? (1 Peter 2:24.) Do you believe it one day and then start doubting it is true the next? That isn't holding fast to your confession. The apostle James warns us about being double minded in this Scripture:

> *But let him ask in faith, with no doubting, for he who doubts is like a wave of the sea driven and tossed by the wind. For let not that man suppose that he will receive anything from the Lord; he is a double-minded man, unstable in all his ways.*

> JAMES 1:6-8 NKJV

You have to hold fast to every promise He has made, that it will be manifested in your life regardless of how the circumstances appear to be. His Word is true, and He doesn't lie. Holding fast to the confession of your faith is a tool, a weapon.

The Power of Agreement

We didn't call people and ask for money, but we did call and ask them to come into agreement with us in prayer for every need. We need the body of Christ to gather around us when we are walking through the desert or through the fire. This isn't a time to let pride keep us isolated. Coming into agreement multiplies the power of our faith. We need each other, as it says here:

> *How should one chase a thousand, and two put ten thousand to flight, except their Rock had sold them, and the Lord had shut them up?*
>
> DEUTERONOMY 32:30

God began to speak to the hearts of people to give and to come alongside us. We were getting off an airplane one day and a pilot stopped me and said, "I'm going to get thirty men to give $500 each for a total of $15,000 for Gabrielle." I don't know if he got the thirty men, but a $15,000 check came in the mail.

A pastor from Jackson, Mississippi, called and said, "I was a police officer in Houston, and I'll come to drive you around while you are at the clinic." This was a blessing because we didn't know our way around the city, and all we had to drive was the big motor coach.

The harvest continued to come in. On the day of Gabrielle's home-going, Terry Law came to our house directly from the airport and handed us a check for $1000. It was a sign from the Lord that said, *I'm not stopping.*

When Richard and I went to the funeral home to make arrangements, the funeral home director said, "The owners of the funeral home called and said to tell you they are personally taking care of the charges for your daughter's funeral." They provided the best of everything.

At the cemetery the man handed me a piece of paper, and I was surprised to see it was in my handwriting. He said, "Yes, this is from when you took care of Mr. Roberts' son." (I had made the arrangements for Richard and

Lindsay when their infant son had gone home to be with Jesus several years earlier.) The man said, "By the way, our board of directors met this morning, and the only thing you have to pay for is the grave marker. We don't do that here, but we are taking care of everything else."

Since Gabrielle's home-going, amazing things have been happening at the services when we minister. While we are teaching and ministering, people start walking up and placing offerings on the platform at our feet totally unsolicited. God truly has opened the windows of heaven.

What have you been planting in your spiritual garden lately? Are you planting good seed in fertile ground? What do you have in your garden that you can give away to others? These are questions you need to examine to determine what type of harvest you can expect. God doesn't expect you to do it alone, and He has given you the weapons and tools you need to plant, cultivate and harvest your garden. Clap your hands and praise Him; pray in the Spirit, wash yourself in the Word of God and put on your armor every day; come into agreement with others of like faith; tithe and give offerings and hold fast to the confession of your faith. When you have done all these, stand on the promises of God. Your harvest is guaranteed!

Angel on Loan

by Paulette (Prewitt) Jones

Our family has been blessed by the fact that tragedy has escaped us for a very long time. Oh, we've had a few deaths, such as my father's and a few uncles', but they had lived reasonably long lives. As a family we were emotionally unprepared to deal with the tragedy of losing one so young and so dear as Gabrielle. We pulled together in seeking God's face, but even then we were in shock as to how and why this happened to one so innocent, precious and pure.

When we visited Gabrielle after she started her treatments, I was so impressed with her sweetness and obvious grasp of the situation. She never complained, although she had every right to do so. She always considered her cousin, Alana, who was eighteen months younger. Gabrielle allowed Alana to play with her toys, even when she was unable to play with them herself. She even tried to teach Alana how to color, draw pictures and paint so they could play together. She always kept her sense of humor and laughed at jokes and funny things on the television. Most of all, I remember how she never forgot to tell me how much she loved me and drew pictures that said, "I love you, Aunt Paulette." In fact, she drew "I love you" pictures for all of the relatives. Somehow, I wonder if subconsciously she knew her life on this earth was going to be short.

The family rallied in faith believing for this miracle for Gabrielle. God has performed so many miracles in our family that we naturally expected another, but that wasn't part of His plan this time. A few days before Gabrielle left us, God revealed to me through my prayers that it was time for Gabrielle to go home to be with Him. I questioned this because I thought we had done everything right in order to receive a miracle. He assured me that it was simply time for her to return home because she was A.O.L.

I was puzzled by this last statement. What did "A.O.L." mean? He told me that Gabrielle was born because of Harry and Cheryl's tremendous faith. I remembered Cheryl almost losing Gabrielle when she was only a few months pregnant. Because of their faith, the baby was not aborted and a few months later Gabrielle was born. God said she was an angel-on-loan from heaven.

Out of this near tragedy, a beautiful, sweet angel was born—an angel who touched the world with her loving nature and sweet voice. But, as He said, it was now time for her to go home. Remember, years in the span of a lifetime are but a moment in heaven. We were blessed to have her with us for six years. All who came in contact with her were blessed just from having known her, our angel-on-loan from heaven, Gabrielle Christian Salem.

But Why, God?

by Cheryl Salem

Have you ever tried to answer a child's question and been bombarded with the classic "but why?" after you've given him what you've thought was a reasonable answer? You try again and again, but he isn't satisfied and keeps coming back at you with a whining, "But why?" Finally in frustration your response is an emphatic, "Because I said so!" Our Father God must feel the same way when His children bombard Him with this "but why" question whenever life isn't going the way they want it to go or whenever they are faced with a crisis or painful event.

It is a natural reaction to want to know why something bad is happening. Even Jesus asked *why* as He hung on the cross. Remember Jesus was a man, and in His humanness He wanted to know *why*. Let's read exactly what He said:

And about the ninth hour Jesus cried out with a loud voice, saying, "Eli, Eli, lama sabachthani?" that is, "My God, My God, why have You forsaken Me?"

MATTHEW 27:46 NKJV

A Question God Won't Answer

The important thing to notice about this is that God did not answer Him. In fact, in any Scripture you read where someone asks God that "but why" question, He never answers the question.

When God appeared to Gideon in the winepress, Gideon posed the "but why" question in this way:

The angel of the Lord came and sat down under the oak in Ophrah that belonged to Joash the Abiezrite, where his son Gideon was threshing wheat in a winepress to keep it from the Midianites. When the angel of the Lord appeared to Gideon, he said, "The Lord is with you, mighty warrior."

"But sir," Gideon replied, "if the Lord is with us, why has all this happened to us? Where are all his wonders that our fathers told us about when they said, `Did not the Lord bring us up out of Egypt?' But now the Lord has abandoned us and put us into the hand of Midian."

The Lord turned to him and said, "Go in the strength you have and save Israel out of Midian's hand. Am I not sending you?"

"But Lord," Gideon asked, "how can I save Israel? My clan is the weakest in Manasseh, and I am the least in my family."

The Lord answered, "I will be with you, and you will strike down all the Midianites together."

JUDGES 6:11-16 NIV

107

The Lord never answered the "but why" questions Gideon asked. God simply encouraged Gideon to do what He was telling him to do and reassured him that He would be with him all the way through to victory.

I believe the reason God doesn't answer such questions is that He knows we can't comprehend with our minute human minds His infinite answer. However, He does promise to walk with us and see us through to victory.

He Will See You Through

After Gabrielle's graduation to heaven, I cried out to the Lord and said, "Why did this have to happen to Gabrielle?" Any parent who loses a child wants to know "why?"

The Lord lovingly responded to my cry and said, *Cheryl, I could come down and stand right in front of you and answer this question; but if I did, because you are a mother in the earthly realm, when I finished telling you the answer, you would turn right around and say again, "But why, Father?" For every answer I gave you, you would still ask, "But why?" Doesn't this sound familiar to you?*

"Yes, it sounds like me with my own children. I can't ever seem to give them an answer that satisfies, and they always have to come back with 'Why? Why? Why?'"

And what do you eventually tell them?

"Because I said so."

Cheryl, that is My answer to you: because I said so! You're going to have to learn to trust Me. You have to go past your faith and step into a new level of trust. When you don't understand, trust Me! When you don't have the answer, trust Me! When you don't know what I'm doing, trust Me!

Step Up to a New Level

It wasn't easy, but I knew I had to do what the Lord said, because getting caught up in the "but why" question would have held me in captivity. I knew in my heart that no matter what explanation the Lord tried to give me, it wouldn't be good enough to satisfy the longing of a mother's heart for her child.

I knew in my heart that no matter what explanation the Lord tried to give me, it wouldn't be good enough to satisfy the longing of a mother's heart for her child.

Stay Out of Captivity

I began to search and study the Hebrew word for "why." The Hebrew language is made up of symbols, and there is one common symbol for "why, when, what, where, who and how much." That symbol means "chaos." When you start asking questions that have no answers and you won't release the circumstances to God, you get yourself into captivity to the spirit of chaos, which brings with it confusion, strife and every evil work. You have to bring your mind under subjection and say, "Lord, I'm going to trust You no matter

109

what. Lord, I'm going to trust You, even if I don't understand."

God knows best, and He knows there are some things we cannot handle.

God knows best, and He knows there are some things we cannot handle. We have had some people say to us, "Well, the reason God took Gabrielle home was so you could have a more powerful worldwide ministry." Harry and I could never receive that as a reason for losing our daughter. We would take having our daughter any day over having a worldwide ministry.

We must get over having to have an answer for everything. There are some things we will never know because, as it says in Deuteronomy 29:29 NKJV, **The secret things belong to the Lord our God.**

Just Trust Him

In the movie *A Few Good Men*, Jack Nicholson plays a hard-core Marine colonel accused of causing the death of a soldier by ordering an illegal "Code Red." Tom Cruise plays the young prosecuting attorney at the trial who hammers the colonel for an answer, saying, "I want to know if you ordered a Code Red?"

Nicholson responds, "You don't want to know."

"I want an answer."

"You don't want an answer."

"I want to know *why* you ordered a Code Red."

"You don't want to know."

"I want the truth!"

"You can't *handle* the truth!"

That is the way God is. He knows we can't handle the answers to our questions, because we can't understand eternal truths with our earthly minds. Asking *why* is an irrelevant question that leads to chaos if we don't let go of it. Chaos leads to captivity, which leads to isolation then desolation and finally devastation, which is a dangerous, lonely place to be when you are in mourning. Let go of the "why?" and let God heal and restore you.

Chaos leads to captivity, which leads to isolation then desolation and finally devastation, which is a dangerous, lonely place to be when you are in mourning.

Here is some godly wisdom I have learned through all of this: Your natural man *wants* an answer; your spirit man *knows* the answer. Your natural man is the one who is grieving; your spirit man knows it is okay.

Focus on the Who!

When Gabrielle became sick and we heard the evil report from the doctors, we knew we had to turn to our Father in heaven. No one else had any answers or any hope. We knew He would lead us, guide us and direct us every step of the way. If we had focused on the *why*, we would never have focused on the who—Jesus, the Healer and Restorer.

If we had focused on the why, we would never have focused on the who—Jesus, the Healer and Restorer.

Now we don't even try to make sense of it. We know there is a reason we had to go through it, and for that reason alone, we trust God. In spite of it all, we trust Him from beginning to end. The Salem family stands on the words spoken by Job when answering his critics, as recorded in this Scripture:

Though He slay me, yet will I trust Him.

JOB 13:15 NKJV

We learned that faith and trust are intertwined. No matter what we go through, to the very brink of death and beyond, we will serve Him, as this Scripture says:

And they overcame him by the blood of the Lamb and by the word of their testimony, and they did not love their lives to the death.

REVELATION 12:11 NKJV

God Is Still God!

by Kenneth Hagin, Jr.

How do we learn to cope with life's problems when things have gone wrong? What do we do? What do we do when Gabrielle didn't seemingly receive what we thought she should receive? How do we face unexpected death? What is our stand?

These are questions people really don't like to face. Many pastors don't like to deal with them either. But it's in situations such as these that we find out whether we really believe God, or simply mouth the words. As we deal with these questions of life, we cannot ask, "Why? Why? Why? Why?" We cannot ask, "Where was Gabrielle's guardian angel?" or anything else like that. The one thing we must do is clearly stated in Scripture:

Trust in the Lord with all thine heart; and lean not unto thine own understanding.

PROVERBS 3:5

Gabrielle made that decision a long, long time ago. She had the strongest faith of any child I've seen, and she would permit no negative thought around her whatsoever. If anyone came around and halfway hinted toward doubt and negativity, she would simply ask her parents to make the person leave.

Gabrielle knew from where her strength came. She knew God intimately. She served God and did more for Him in six years than some people do in seventy. She was a little girl who was way beyond her years. Her life was to sing for God. That's all she really wanted to do—sing for the Lord.

I believe she recognized these talents were a special gift from God early on and made a decision to do everything she could to promote God and His kingdom. She began playing the piano when she was two and began singing with almost perfect pitch at three years of age. Then she began to minister with the family and used this gift to tell them when they had missed a note or two.

As we were getting ready to come in for Gabby's home-going celebration, I asked Harry and Cheryl and the boys, "Have you checked yourself over?" That's what Gabby would have done, looked them over to make sure everybody had everything just right before going out on the stage. She demanded perfection of herself and of others.

I remember well the last time that she sang on a church platform. It was at our church, Rhema Bible Church, in May of 1999. She came into the speaker's room very, very ill, with her little *Bug's Life* backpack that she carried her IV's around in.

Harry spoke to her and said, "It's okay if you stay here in the back room and watch us on the television." With indignation, she looked at him as if to say, *What are you talking about, "stay in the back room"?* She picked up that little backpack, headed for that platform and said, "I'm *going* to sing!" I remember that she was very upset because the soundman didn't have her track loud enough. She was concerned that she might sing off-key because she couldn't hear her track. Once again, that was her perfection coming out. She was so sick she had to leave immediately after singing, but she refused to give up.

In her fight of faith, Gabrielle trusted in God all the way. All of us need to learn, as Gabrielle did, to lean not on our own understanding, but to trust in the Lord.

In our lives, we are going to face situations in which we must make a choice. Is God still God, or is He just God when everything's going well and when there is no adversity? I have to tell you God is still God regardless of our circumstances, because the Word of God says He is, as in Genesis 35:11: **I *am* God Almighty.**

Gabrielle made her choice a long time ago. She knew that God must be God at all times: when she was playing, when she was on the platform ministering, when she was coloring or drawing a picture. To her, God was there all the time. God was God in all places, under all circumstances— whether good or bad. God was still God.

That is the decision each of us needs to make today. God is still God in the good times and in the bad times. Once you make that decision, you won't have problems with any more questions. When you make the choice to lean not to your own understanding but to trust in God, you can face the adversities of life without wavering. When a storm comes on the ocean of life, you can sail right through it, because God is God and He always will be God.

What did Jesus do when He faced an adversity in His own country where He'd grown up? Did He get offended and walk away? The Scripture says this:

> *Now He could do no mighty work there, except that He laid His hands on a few sick people and healed them. And He marveled because of their unbelief. Then He went about the villages in a circuit, teaching.*

> MARK 6:5,6 NKJV

No, He left there and went to the surrounding villages, cities and towns teaching and preaching and healing.

So what should we make up our minds to do today? We should make up our minds that God is still God and decide to go on doing what He did: preaching and teaching and healing.

A big part of coming out of a tragedy or a defeat rests in your decision—what you decide to do. I trust that you will decide to do what Gabrielle did: "Trust in the Lord with all your heart and lean not to your own understanding."

It's in times like these that we find out whether we really believe or not. Some would say, "I don't understand." Neither do I. Some would say, "Pastor, do you have the answer?" No, I don't have *the* answer, but I have *an* answer and this is it: If we allow the enemy to take this battle and win, we lose the war. It is up to us to make something good come out of this. It is up to us to raze hell, to tear down the devil's kingdom. That's what Gabrielle did, and that's what she would love for us to do.

No, we don't understand everything; and we never will. I've heard my father say this ever since I can remember: "Son, always take a negative and make a positive out of it in everything you do." Gabrielle's home-going is not a negative. It is a positive. And what you do with it will determine *how* positive it will be.

The apostle Paul said,

For now we see through a glass, darkly; but then face to face: now I know in part; but then shall I know even as also I am known.

1 CORINTHIANS 13:12

We don't know everything. We don't understand everything. But I do know this: I refuse to quit, and I cannot be defeated.

Where there is faith, there is love. Where there is faith, there is peace. Where there is faith, there is deliverance. Where there is faith, there is life evermore. Not to move on in God and not to continue to stand strong in our faith, as Gabrielle did, would allow the enemy to win the war. I don't intend to do that myself. I intend to come off the canvas and deck him. I intend to reach out and snatch those from the devil's kingdom and transfer them into the kingdom of light.

Today if Gabrielle could speak, I believe she would say, "Will you please make the decision I made and go and do something for God?" Will you do it?

Keeping the Balance
of Faith and Trust

by Cheryl Salem

Have you ever heard that old song that goes, "Love and marriage, love and marriage, go together like a horse and carriage; this I tell you, brother, you can't have one without the other"? Faith and trust are the same way: You can't have one without the other. We stood in faith for Gabrielle's healing and restoration. Without an equal amount of trust in the Lord, our faith might have been shattered when God didn't do it the way we expected or wanted Him to do it. He did it His way and for His reasons, which we may never understand. But He did it!

With all the miracles I have experienced in my own life, I know what it takes to stand in faith without wavering. It is an immediate response to every trial in my life, and the battle for Gabrielle's life was no different. With the tenacity of a bulldog we went to war using all the weapons God has given us. But I have learned one thing about my walk with God: He requires humility and total submission to Him as He takes us from faith to faith. Every situation is different, and He always has a new lesson for us to learn.

God wanted me to learn how important it is to have the proper balance of faith and trust, because when we get out of balance, faith can actually become an idol.

Balance Is the Key

In my case, God wanted me to learn how important it is to have the proper balance of faith and trust, because when we get out of balance, faith can actually become an idol. The Lord kept speaking these two Scriptures to me over and over, and I just didn't get what He was saying:

For I am the Lord Who heals you.

EXODUS 15:26 NKJV

and

You shall have no other gods before Me

EXODUS 20:3 NKJV

Through the months of caring for Gabrielle, the Lord taught me several valuable lessons about this. With the IV running almost continuously and our pushing her to drink huge amounts of water to flush out her body, Gabrielle had to go potty almost every fifteen minutes. This went on day and night. She was up and down, and so was I. When Gabrielle went back to sleep, I took out my Bible and started confessing the Word over her. After several weeks with little or no sleep, I was exhausted. Finally one night God and I had this conversation:

"I'm so sleepy."

Go to sleep!

"I've got to speak the Word over my daughter: 'She will live and not die and proclaim the works of the Lord...'"

In mid-sentence He stopped me and said, *How many times do you think you have said that over her in her lifetime?*

"I don't know—maybe 1000 times."

Don't you know that once the Word is spoken into the heavens, it never stops working? The Word never loses its power. It never stops. So go to sleep. You've got enough Word in the atmosphere to heal the whole world!

God knew I couldn't go on at the pace I was going, and He gently and lovingly corrected me that night. I was trying to do everything in my own power and strength, and I was taking a burden on myself that was not mine to carry. By golly, I was going to be sure she was healed by the words of *my* mouth, even if it killed me. My faith was out of balance, and I was making my confession of faith—the process of speaking the Word—into an idol. I continued to speak the Word over Gabrielle—but not at the expense of my own rest and health. I had peace knowing God's Word was active whether I was awake or asleep.

Beware of Idols

I begged the Lord for more revelation and insight to show me any other idols in which I was placing my faith. One big one that every parent faces when dealing with a critically ill child is making medical decisions. What is the best treatment? If I make this decision, will it kill her? Is she getting too much of this medicine or not enough? Is she eating the right food? Is she drinking enough water? It went on and on, and each day I had to examine in whom or what I was placing my faith. Was I trusting God to heal, or was I trying to do it for Him? Was I looking to the doctors and medicine to do it? Most importantly, was I allowing Satan to bring fear, guilt and condemnation on me about the decisions we had to make?

Let Peace Rule Your Heart

Harry and I learned that when we put our faith in the Lord to do the healing, peace ruled in our hearts regarding all the difficult decisions. The greatest test of this came in July 1999 in Michigan. We had been ministering at several churches and visiting some of Harry's family. Harry's sister,

Stephanie, took Gabrielle and the boys to visit some of the relatives one afternoon. They rode go-carts. Gabrielle had the time of her life, but she came back to the room that night complaining of a headache. The next morning we went to preach. Gabrielle stayed at the room with Tracey. When we came back from the service, she still had the headache.

When we put our faith in the Lord to do the healing, peace ruled in our hearts regarding all the difficult decisions.

Harry and I felt an urgency to head for home. Gabrielle was in trouble, and we knew it. She was in considerable pain from the headache, and she was drooling uncontrollably. We loaded up the motor coach and headed for Tulsa. As we headed down the interstate, Gabrielle was getting worse every minute. I was trying not to panic or get into fear, but I knew I was losing her when she started turning blue and becoming unresponsive. I finally got one of the doctors from the Houston clinic on the phone, and she said to find the closest emergency room. We were near St. Joseph, Michigan, and didn't know where to find a hospital, so Harry called a nearby church where we had once ministered. The associate pastor who answered said they had been praying for our family and then said, "I will meet you at the St. Joseph's exit."

He met us, and we followed him through town, bolting through all the lights and pulling up right at the emergency room entrance. He had called ahead and alerted the emergency room staff that we were coming. As Harry opened the door to the motor coach, this pastor who was large in stature jumped in, picked Gabrielle up as though she was as light as a feather and carried her to the waiting gurney.

The nurses rushed her into the exam room and a doctor immediately intubated her, as she wasn't breathing. The ER staff went into action running tests, including a CT scan. The doctor came out and said, "It appears the left ventricle of her brain is blocked, and she needs surgery. We are going to have to Life Flight her to Kalamazoo, Michigan. If we don't do surgery, she's got two hours."

When we first heard that she had two hours to live, we started to panic. We had to kill a lot of gods that day, from the doctors to the diagnosis to the CT scans. In the very beginning of Gabrielle's illness, the Lord had spoken to me and said, "When Gabrielle gets through this, she won't even smell of smoke!" Harry and I prayed and did not feel that the Lord wanted us to authorize surgery. We still believed that even in the midst of this crisis, God was going to heal her.

When Harry told the doctor our decision not to do surgery, the doctor said, "Do you understand the consequences?"

"Yes, we do."

"I respect that, but we still need to Life Flight her to the Pediatric Intensive Care Unit in Kalamazoo."

We watched them load our daughter on the gurney, and someone said, "You need to say good-bye to her.

Harry said, "This is not good-bye." He leaned down and whispered to Gabrielle, who was unconscious, "We'll see you soon."

We stood in the parking lot and watched them load the gurney onto the helicopter. They wouldn't let me go with her. I thought at that moment I would die from the separation. Harry was holding the boys, and with tears streaming down his cheeks, Little Harry said, "Is she going to die?"

Harry said, "No!"

Right then we had an opportunity to come into agreement with death, but we rebuked it. We trusted God, totally committed our precious little one to Him and said, "God, You have to take care of her on this helicopter."

It was a thirteen-minute flight to Kalamazoo. We got in the motor coach and headed for the hospital. Our cell phone started ringing. Pastor Dave Williams from Lansing called and said, "I'm standing in the emergency room in Kalamazoo. When she wakes up, she will recognize my face and won't be scared or alone." Another pastor called and said, "I'm standing on the helipad." I don't know how these people found out so quickly, but when we arrived, there were already three pastors and their wives waiting for us. Gabrielle was never alone, and neither were we. A total of sixteen pastors and their wives came to the hospital to be with us that night.

The neurosurgeon came to talk with us. He showed us the CT scan and said, "You understand without surgery the swelling may stop her breathing and her heart? She won't make it through the night."

"Yes, we understand."

We sat with her all night with the ventilator hissing and all the tubes coming out of her body. Everyone was praying. She made it through the night. In the morning, they did an MRI. We waited through the day for a report and prayed.

At eight o'clock that night, the doctor *finally* came to get us. We had to walk down a long corridor, around the back of the cafeteria and down another dark hallway to get to a small room where we could look at the MRI. We felt as though we had walked into the valley of the shadow of death right there in the darkness. The doctor turned on the light screen and said, "Well, here is the tumor...I don't know what they diagnosed last night, but what I see here looks like mini strokes. The pre-described surgery would not have helped."

We knew we had heard from God regarding the surgery. We said, "She's trying to wake up and come out of this coma."

"Well, let's go wake her up."

We went back to the intensive care unit, and they woke her up. We asked them if they were going to take the ventilator tube out, and the doctor said, "No, I don't think she can breathe without it." But Gabrielle was pointing at it as if to say, "You either take it out, or I'm ripping it out." They took it out.

The next morning we knew we had our miracle when the doctor said, "You can take her home, but you can't ride in the motor coach. You'll have to fly."

Let Go and Let God!

Harry began trying to find an airplane to charter to take her home, but he hit a wall on every turn. One plane had taken off but had to return to the airport because of mechanical problems. Two others were already in service in different parts of the country. It just seemed futile. Someone suggested Life Flight, but the thirteen-minute flight had cost $8000, and Harry decided to keep trying other alternatives. Richard was on the phone in Tulsa as well. Things looked hopeless, and I finally said to Harry, "Let's stop trying to do this, and let God do it!"

A little while later, Harry received phone calls from two men we don't even know, who each offered to make his airplane available. One was in Atlanta, and one was in Michigan. Harry walked in the room to tell me just as I hung up the phone. I said, "Kenneth Copeland's airplane has been in the air for the last forty minutes." Thank God, He had it under control!

Amazing Grace

Gabrielle amazed the doctors because she had no residual effects from the mini strokes. She came home and sat in our bed talking and singing, playing her little keyboard, coloring and playing with her Barbie's.

The challenge we faced after returning home from this crisis was whether or not to continue the experimental treatment with the clinic in Houston. The treatment was not getting the response we had hoped for, and the steroids and terrible weight gain caused all sorts of problems. We prayed and felt it was time to stop the treatment and to wean her off the huge doses of steroids she was on. We could no longer put our faith in the treatment and in the medicine. It was not working; it was not even helping. We were confident in God's healing process. The next MRI showed some improvement over the one taken in Michigan.

One More Journey

As the months from July to November moved along, we continued to valiantly fight the battle for Gabrielle's healing and restoration. We stayed at home during the remainder of July and through August. On Labor Day weekend we were able to go to Memphis and minister. In October we began a swing through the southern states and did two engagements in Alabama before returning home with Gabrielle one last time.

Our faith was definitely focused on the substance of things hoped for and the evidence of things not seen, as

Hebrews 11:1 says. We weren't seeing any evidence of the manifestation of her healing, but we continued the confession of our faith by speaking the Word of God over Gabrielle. Her faith was even more unstoppable than ours. She said, "I'm so glad we came on this trip to see Pastor Fred and Valerie. I'm having fun again!"

Faith is the single most creative force that God has given us on the face of this earth.

Faith is a powerful weapon and is strong enough to move mountains, tear down city walls, close lions' mouths, subdue kingdoms, produce strength out of weakness and raise the dead. Faith is the single most creative force that God has given us on the face of this earth. The greatest gift He has given us that makes us the most like Him is our ability to speak His Word and to pray things into existence.

God Is Sovereign

There was a time when I believed we could change *anything* with our words, by our prayers and by our faith. However, as God has taken us up another faith level through this experience with Gabrielle, I now understand better the fine line between faith and trust. We can't have one without the other. God has a sovereign plan that cannot be thwarted by our wants and desires. Does this mean we never believe God for anything again? No, it means we believe God wholeheartedly for *everything*, which includes trusting Him that whatever the outcome, it is His very best for us. Truly, all things do work together for our good, as we have read in this Scripture so many times:

> *We are assured and know that [God being a partner in their labor] all things work together and are [fitting into a plan] for good to and for those who love God and are called according to [His] design and purpose.*
>
> ROMANS 8:28 AMP

This is not just a trite statement to make someone feel better when going through a trial. God's Word is truth, *and it is life.* The eighth chapter of Romans is a metaphor of how to live a resurrected life in Christ. If we love Him and are called by Him to do His purpose, we can trust Him (and His plan) in *all* things. This is the balance between faith and trust. This is why Harry and I can truthfully say our faith did not fail us when Gabrielle graduated to heaven sooner than we wanted. God answered our prayers. He simply did it His way.

God has a sovereign plan that cannot be thwarted by our wants and desires.

Faith Does Not Fail

Not long after Gabrielle's home-going, we were flying to a ministry engagement and the pilot came back to speak with us. He said, "The first thing I'm going to do when I get to heaven is to ask God why your daughter didn't get healed."

Harry said, "No, you're not, because when you get to heaven and see our little girl totally restored at thirty-seven pounds with shining blue eyes and blond hair blowing in the breeze, you aren't going to ask any questions whatsoever. You'll know she got both healed *and* restored!"

The devil plays havoc with people's minds when they have their faith and trust out of balance.

We have an entire race of *faith* people who walk around carrying the biggest pile of guilt on their heads because they didn't get what they prayed for and believed God would do. Of course, we know guilt and condemnation don't come from God. The devil plays havoc with people's minds when they have their faith and trust out of balance. It is the major cause for people turning their backs on God when bad things happen.

As we travel, people come up to us and marvel at our faith. In June 1999 after visiting our home and praying, Benny Hinn said he never saw a family with such faith. He and Suzanne had come bringing gifts and words of faith, support and encouragement. They walked away shaking their heads and marveling at the committed, determined faith of a little six-year-old girl and her family. We don't share this to elevate ourselves above others. We want people to know that faith works when it is balanced with trust.

His Promises Link to His Purposes

How do we know this? Because God's promises are linked to His purposes, and His purposes are guaranteed: He never fails. God's purposes depend solely on Him and cannot be stopped, and His purposes are to have a people of faith who trust His promises even though they may not line up with man's expectations.[1] These passages of Scripture prove these statements:

> *Praised (honored, blessed) be the God and Father of our Lord Jesus Christ (the Messiah)! By His boundless mercy we have been born again to an ever-living hope through the resurrection of Jesus Christ from the dead, [born anew] into an inheritance which is beyond the reach of change and decay [imperishable], unsullied and unfading, reserved in heaven for you, who are being guarded (garrisoned) by God's power through [your] faith [till you fully inherit that final] salvation that is ready to be revealed [for you] in the last time.*
>
> *[You should] be exceedingly glad on this account, though now for a little while you may be distressed by trials and suffer temptations, so that [the genuineness] of your faith may be tested, [your faith] which is infinitely more precious than the perishable gold which is tested and purified by fire. [This proving of your faith is intended] to redound to [your] praise and glory and honor when Jesus Christ (the Messiah, the Anointed One) is revealed. Without having seen Him, you love Him; though you do not [even] now see Him, you believe in Him and exult and thrill with inexpressible and glorious*

131

(triumphant, heavenly) joy. [At the same time] you receive the result (outcome, consummation) of your faith, the salvation of your souls.

The prophets, who prophesied of the grace (divine blessing) which was intended for you, searched and inquired earnestly about this salvation. They sought [to find out] to whom or when this was to come which the Spirit of Christ working within them was indicating when he predicted the sufferings of Christ and the glories that should follow [them].

1 PETER 1:3-11 AMP

However, it is not as though God's Word had failed [come to nothing].

ROMANS 9:6 AMP

We did what we knew to do, and God did what He said He would do.

Trust in the One Who Holds the Keys

We had confidence in the One who promises, and we trusted Him to fulfill what He had promised. We did what we knew to do, and God did what He said He would do. Our faith overcame the onslaught of the enemy, and our trust in Almighty God allows us to walk in victory. Would we do the same thing again? Absolutely, only we would do it better because our faith is stronger than ever. We are secure in who we are in Christ and, therefore, are able to allow our expectations to be changed for His purposes, and we have learned the value of trusting the One who holds the keys to the resurrected life.

The Face of Faith

by Richard and Lindsay Roberts

If faith had a face, it would look like Gabrielle!

We have been through death, debt, destruction, devastation and much more in over twenty years of marriage, but nothing could compare to what we experienced from January 11, 1999, to November 23, 1999. Whether we live a million years or the Lord returns tomorrow, nothing can feel like what we felt on January 11, 1999, our twentieth wedding anniversary.

Lindsay and I had no real celebration planned. In fact, our anniversary had always been a family thing; and this night was no different. However, it turned out to be very different when Harry and Cheryl called and asked us to meet them at our home immediately. There was no way to prepare for what they were about to tell us.

The previous night would prove to have been prophetic, disturbing, revealing and a host of other things as the Lord had awakened Lindsay and told her to pray. The news she would hear would be about Gabrielle and a tumor. However, nothing hit our souls like hearing the words, "Gabrielle" and "tumor" in the same sentence as it rolled out of Harry and Cheryl's mouths.

The room was filled with shock and faith at the same time. Human emotions were coupled with God-like faith that touched the heart of the Father. As you will discover throughout this book, there are many details of this story— some so devastating, it is beyond belief how human beings can experience them and yet still live through them. However, we want to go outside the realm of the natural events and give you our insight on what we experienced. We witnessed a dimension in the supernatural realm of the God-kind of faith we read about, as in the following Scripture, but rarely have the privilege of seeing in the flesh:

> *So Jesus answered and said to them, "Have faith in God. For assuredly, I say to you, whoever says to this mountain, 'Be removed and be cast into the sea,' and does not doubt in his heart, but believes that those things he says will be done, he will have whatever he says. Therefore I say to you, whatever things you ask when you pray, believe that you receive them, and you will have them.*

MARK 11:22-24 NKJV

Harry and Cheryl Salem had spent years training their children in faith. Discipline means to make a disciple of one by training or by example, and this was *exactly* what they had lived—training by example. From years of living "on the road" in a motor home, traveling border-to-border, coast-to-coast, proclaiming the Gospel of Jesus Christ, their children learned an enormous amount about faith from both experience and simple *absorption*, which comes by hearing the Word of God, as it says in this Scripture:

> *So faith comes by hearing [what is told], and what is heard*
> *comes by the preaching [of the message that came from the*
> *lips] of Christ (the Messiah Himself).*
>
> ROMANS 10:17 AMP

This faith was forced into action in demonstration, the likes of which we have never seen before. Some have said, "But Gabrielle went to heaven." Yes, that is true, but just because her journey here on earth was complete, it does *not* in any way change faith from being faith.

Faith is not the manipulation of a wishy-washy God in order to get the desired result of your choosing. Faith is *pure* and absolute trust in an almighty God, no matter the result of any situation—your way or not. Faith is trusting His way *at all cost!* And sometimes it costs you everything—even your very life.

In one Bible version the subtitle for the eleventh chapter of Hebrews reads, "Heroes of Faith," and verse 13 NKJV says, **These all died in faith.** Now, that may seem to be a great contradiction to the statement "If you had any faith, a person wouldn't die." That's not what Hebrews 11 says; and since God wrote it, He's the final authority. There are heroes-of-faith generals in the army of God who finish their courses and receive their heavenly rewards. I don't believe we, as humans, can judge a long life or a productive life in terms of the number of years lived. God made it quite clear that His ways and thoughts are different from ours in this Scripture:

> *For as the heavens are higher than the earth, so are My ways*
> *higher than your ways, and My thoughts than your thoughts.*
>
> ISAIAH 55:9 NKJV

Therefore, it is not up to us to decide how God operates or how He thinks.

Faith is an unwavering trust in the almighty God, who knows and sees everything—even the beginning and the end. I have never seen such unfailing, unstaggering, unshakable faith in the midst of the fiery trials of life demonstrated like this before. Perhaps it was Gabrielle's training, perhaps it was her child-like trust or perhaps it was a sovereign gift from a merciful God, but this child *never* changed her opinion of God even for so much as a *split second.* Oh, to have that kind of child-like faith as an adult! That would be perhaps one of the greatest gifts our God could give!

Faith was Gabrielle's essence, her fiber, her DNA to the innermost part of her existence. And the only thing of equal magnitude she demonstrated daily was the gift of joy. If, as Nehemiah 8:10 declares, **The joy of the Lord is your strength,** then Gabrielle is truly the *strongest* person we have ever known.

Joy is not happy or sad, up or down, traveling on the emotional roller coaster of life through some journey or totally dependent on circumstances. Joy is a spirit—that outward manifestation of an inward strength that can come only from the hand of God. It defies emotion, supersedes circumstances and overcomes obstacles as only the supernatural power of God can do. As far as joy can be described, Gabrielle put flesh and bones and blood and tissue to a word few ever know in this dimension. Gabrielle *was* joy!

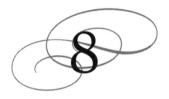

Facing the Memories

by Cheryl Salem

The death of a child, no matter at what age, has to be one of the deepest pains anyone experiences. No one can possibly comprehend it until he or she has walked through it, and not one experience is exactly the same as another. There is an old saying that goes something like this: "Never judge a man until you have walked a mile in his shoes." Harry and I appreciate this saying so much more since we walked through the most painful year of our lives. We now have a greater compassion for those who are caretakers and/or have experienced the death of someone they love. We also have a deeper appreciation for what our heavenly Father did when He sent His own Son to be sacrificed for our sins.

Hope Reaches Beyond the Grave

It is unnatural for a parent to have to bury a child. It doesn't line up with the scheme of life. It begets grief beyond comprehension, but it is not without hope for those who are in Christ Jesus. The Word is very specific about this, as it says in this Scripture:

> *Now also we would not have you ignorant, brethren, about those who fall asleep [in death], that you may not grieve [for them] as the rest do who have no hope [beyond the grave].*

1 THESSALONIANS 4:13 AMP

People come up to us all the time and ask how we have been able to bear the pain. Our only answer is that our hope is in the Lord. We know where Gabrielle is, and we know she is fully restored.

Gabrielle loved to swim. However, once the IV port was inserted into her chest, she wasn't able to go swimming. That was very difficult for her to accept. The morning of her home-going celebration Little Harry asked me what I thought Gabrielle was doing in heaven that morning. I said, "She's probably swimming in the waters of the River of Life and loving every minute of it!"

If we look carefully at the above Scripture, we must conclude that we can't entertain grief and hope at the same time. As Christians we are told not to grieve as the world grieves, because we do have the hope of life beyond the grave. We have hope in knowing that someday we are going to be with Gabrielle again. She isn't dead. She is more alive than she ever was here on earth.

Twin-rooted Spirits

The Lord showed Harry and me that grief and death are twin-rooted spirits. Death comes and goes quickly, but grief stays if we let it. The spirit of grief does not come from God. That means it comes from Satan, and it can be deadly because it attacks your emotions and sucks the very Word—life and breath—of God out of you.

Grief is like a tornado that sweeps down sucking everything in its path up into the funnel cloud spinning off a twin, that is death.

When you live in "tornado alley," as we do in Oklahoma, you learn a lot about tornadoes. The worst kind of tornado is one that goes along a path and spins off a twin. The twin is more violent, unpredictable and destructible than the original storm. Grief is like a tornado that sweeps down sucking everything in its path up into the funnel cloud spinning off a twin, that is death. That is why grief is such a dangerous place.

A week after Gabrielle left us, I became terribly sick and couldn't stop vomiting. In my weakness I was on my knees in the bathroom and said, "Devil, here I am. I make myself a target. *If* you can do it, do it now!"

Three months later, the doctors diagnosed colon cancer. It was a wake-up call for me to get back in the fight. Remember, I said to Satan, *"If you can do it...* He couldn't do it, and I am healed and restored today. Once again, the devil lost!

Do Christian's Grieve?

So you may be asking, "Don't Christian's grieve?" The answer is yes, we do. Grief is an emotion, and it is part of the pain of separation when someone we love is suddenly gone out of our lives. The point I am making, though, is that we are not to grieve as those who have no hope, and we aren't to let grief settle in and become part of our identities.

Grief is an emotion, and it is part of the pain of separation when someone we love is suddenly gone out of our lives.

Kenneth Copeland has written an excellent mini-book titled *Sorrow Not!* In it he shares a story of a woman who allowed uncontrolled grief to gain a foothold in her life. For years she was in such deep sorrow over the death of one of her children that she had not been able to function as a wife or a mother to her other children. When Brother Copeland spoke a word of truth to her at a service one night, she was set free from the grief that had been crippling her. It was the truth of God's Word that set her free.

Reality Versus Truth

When faced with pain and trauma in life, we must learn to differentiate between reality and truth. Reality is that Gabrielle died; the truth is that she is restored and alive. Reality is that we miss Gabrielle terribly; the truth is that it won't be long before we see her again. Here is an example from the Bible: Reality is that Peter walked on the water; the truth is that Jesus kept him afloat. (Matt. 14:28-31.)

Overcoming the Separation

The pain of separation from Gabrielle has been so intense that sometimes it seems unbearable. One day I asked the Lord why we felt the separation so strongly when the spiritual realm is so close. The Lord said it is because of the Fall in the Garden of Eden, when man was separated from God. Otherwise, we would not feel the separation between earth and heaven.

One time I said to the Lord, "If You want to make me happy, then just send her back to me. Do an end-time miracle and send her back to the earth. You raised Lazarus from the grave after four days; and if You want to raise somebody seven months later, I've got the faith for it."

The Lord in His grace answered me and said, *Cheryl, the separation that you feel will not be satisfied by My sending her back to you. The separation will be satisfied when you learn that she won't come down to you, but you must come up to her in the*

Spirit. This sounds a little way out, but let me explain it as He did.

We always say, "Holy Spirit, come down, fall upon us, come into this service, fill up this house."

The Lord said, *All these years I have been trying to get people to come up to Me. I don't want to come down to them. I want them to come up to Me in the spiritual realm. If you want to lessen the feeling of separation, you have to do what it takes to remove yourself from your human feelings and lift yourself up higher on a supernatural level with Me in the Spirit, which is where her spirit is. The way to do this is by praying and staying in My Word so that you are heavenly minded rather than earthly minded. When you are in services ministering, you are heavenly minded and you don't feel the separation.*

That was such a revelation to me. I know it is true, because when I am under the anointing and ministering I don't feel any separation at all. It is when I am tired and allow my mind to roam in the earthly realm of memories that I feel the separation so intensely.

Beware of Deception

Let me share with you what Satan tried to do to me right after Gabrielle went home. I didn't want to pray or read the Word because I thought reading the Word and praying would make me even sadder because it would make me think of Jesus and miss her even more because she is with Him. That is deception in its purest form. Remember what

I said earlier about the spirit of grief sucking the Word out of us?

Develop a Taste for the Word

What added to this was being battle-weary. We had waged a massive war against the enemy for eleven months, fighting death, hell and the grave on all fronts. I was so tired of not sleeping. I was tired of praying and being in the Word. I felt like I just needed a reprieve. This was another tactic of the enemy, because the longer the reprieve I had, the longer I wanted it to last. It's like developing a taste for something and then not having it for a while. You lose your taste for it.

Since my colon surgery I have had to drink a protein drink that is fortified with cod liver oil and all sorts of nutritious supplements. I mix it in the blender with a cup of juice and have tried to disguise the taste every way possible. In the beginning I gagged the whole glass down, but each day it got a little bit better. After drinking it for a month or two, I actually developed a taste for it and looked forward to drinking it.

Recently we were extremely busy with a weeklong conference that had us on the go night and day. I didn't have the time or opportunity to fix my protein drink. By the end of the week, when I mixed up a drink, I found I had lost my taste for it. I had to start all over again.

It was the same way with getting my prayer life and Bible study time back in gear. It took discipline to get back into a routine, but my hunger for His presence increased quickly.

Don't Play Videos of the Past

Another way Satan messes with people who are in mourning is to disrupt their sleep by playing videos of the past over and over in their minds. This is especially true when they have seen someone they love suffer through a painful sickness or a bad accident.

In the beginning it was like I couldn't control the instant replays of the bad memories. Every time I closed my eyes, the tape would start rolling. That was one reason we stayed so busy those first few months. There was a time of grace when God allowed us to be busy so we wouldn't go crazy, but there was no peace in busyness.

It wasn't until I got sick and had to stop traveling and ministering that I had to deal with controlling my mind. In the stillness when the instant replays of bad memories started infiltrating my mind, I prayed and said, "God, You've got to erase this video." He started replacing it with good memories and teaching me to pray in the Spirit, because when you pray in the Spirit, your mind has to turn off. When I prayed in the Spirit, my thoughts came under control. My prayer language has been a powerful weapon against the bad memories.

Facing the memories, both good and bad, has not been easy. Writing this book has been painful and healing at the same time. Reality is that the pain of being separated from Gabrielle is ever present; the truth is that God's grace and mercies give us the strength to push on through it. Grief is like quicksand; it tries to pull you down into the muck and mire. Grief comes, but it is our choice to make it go by keeping our focus both on the reality that Jesus already overcame death, and on the truth that our job is simply to learn how to manage it in a healthy way.

Grief is like quicksand; it tries to pull you down into the muck and mire.

Rebel or Rebound?

by Dave Williams

I was honored to have a part in Gabrielle Christian Salem's home-going celebration service. It was an emotionally and spiritually moving time. Many people had wonderful words to say about this precious six-year-old. I had only known Gabrielle for about eighteen months, but I really loved her. I called her "Gab," and she called me "Pastor Tipover." Of course, there was a story behind that name.

Harry and Cheryl and the family were ministering at our church in Lansing, Michigan, and we took some time for fun in the sun at a nearby lake. Before going to the lake, I confessed to Harry and Cheryl that I had gotten a couple of tattoos while I'd been in the Navy before I had become saved. I told them there were only two rules when we go boating or swimming: (1) no tattoo jokes and (2) no fat jokes! They laughed and made me feel as if it was no big deal.

But to me it *was* a big deal. I hadn't gone swimming with my shirt off for over twenty years, because I was ashamed of the tattoos. I didn't want to be a bad example to young people. Actually, you couldn't even see them when I wore a short-sleeved shirt, which I always did.

Anyway, while I was jet-skiing with Roman, I turned too slowly on the high performance Seadoo, and we tipped over. Thus, I was nicknamed "Pastor Tipover."

Later that same day, Gab was on the pontoon boat and I was on the dock when I noticed the boat was drifting away. I leaned over and grabbed Gab and lifted her over to the dock. I groaned as I felt something pull in my back as I set Gab safely on the dock.

Woman of faith that she is, Cheryl said, "It usually takes me about four days to believe God for a healing when that happens to me." We laughed.

Nonetheless, later that day I lay flat on the floor of the lake cottage and stretched trying to get rid of the pain in my back. I don't know if it was then that Gab first noticed my tattoo, but Cheryl related this conversation to me later.

"Mom, there's a spot on Pastor Tipover's arm."

"Honey, that's a tattoo Pastor Tipover got when he was in the Navy before he knew Jesus."

Gabrielle, very serious and concerned said, "Mom, let's pretend like we didn't notice it, because it might make Pastor Tipover feel bad if he thinks we saw it."

She never mentioned it to me. The boys, on the other hand, were a different story. It didn't bother them to ask what it was. I just told them it was a cartoon, and they'd "better never think about getting one."

We had fun that day. I was liberated from the fear of people knowing about my body art, and the kids all agreed it was the best day in their entire lives. How could we ever imagine that sixteen months later Gabrielle would be in heaven?

She was small, but, oh, what an undeniable anointing she carried. The first time I met her I told Cheryl that Gab had the same type of anointing I had sensed on Kathryn Kuhlman in her services before she went to heaven. That same "sense" came over me whenever I was around Gab.

There were so many touching things about her little life. My heart ached for Harry, Cheryl and the boys when I received the call that she had journeyed on ahead of them to heaven. Yet, I wasn't surprised when Harry and Cheryl came to the platform during the celebration service and affirmed their faith in God and the fact that they were moving ahead with God, in spite of this confusing situation that was so difficult to understand. I knew how solid their faith and trust was in a loving God regardless of the pain they were experiencing in their hearts at that moment.

As a pastor I have seen a great deal of grief and mourning over the years. I have noticed two very different outcomes in the lives of people who experience a loss. They either rebel or rebound. Harry and Cheryl rebounded.

As a young, fifteen-year-old boy who lost his father to a sudden, unexpected death, I was one who rebelled. "What kind of God would kill a forty-year-old man and take him from his loving wife and children?" I questioned. Being raised in a traditional church, we were clueless concerning the true nature and character of God. Thus I rebelled. I quit church and at the age of sixteen started drinking alcohol and doing every wild and corrupt thing I could. I joined the Navy and became even wilder, not wanting anything to do with "the God who killed my dad."

I did not realize that in my rebellion I was actually running *with* the god who killed my dad—the devil. It wasn't until I met some men who knew the Word of God, led me to the authentic Christ and taught me about the wonderful love of the Father God that I learned how wrong I had been. God is good and loving, and the devil is evil and hateful. God didn't kill my dad. I had been deceived and was rebelling against the God who had created me and whose wish was that His people prosper and be in health. (3 John 2.) If I had only known the truth, I could have saved myself from years of dangerous living and a mammoth amount of pain and suffering.

This is what happens when a person suffers a loss or a perceived loss. They rebel or they rebound. Those who don't know and trust in Jesus Christ and His Word usually rebel. Those who do know and trust Jesus Christ rebound and turn out prospering more than ever.

Grief gets a grip through a loss, and it is deadly. Hanging on to grief is like hanging on to a snake's egg. It may feel warm, but eventually that egg will hatch and you won't like the results, as it says in this Scripture:

> *They hatch vipers' eggs and weave the spider's web; he who eats of their eggs dies, and from that which is crushed a viper breaks out.*
>
> ISAIAH 59:5 NKJV

One of the devil's lures is the lure of grief. He uses it to keep people from fulfilling God's purposes in their lives.

Grief is not the same thing as mourning. Grief is something that can drill deep into the heart of a person and can actually change the human personality and create monstrous, abhorrent behavior. Grief brings despair and can even lead to suicide.

When the stock market crashed in 1929, many perceived their losses as irreversible. Even some of Wall Street's best-known, most powerful men took their own lives in despair, grieving over their losses.

On New Year's Day 2000 I read a newspaper article about a twenty-two-year-old man who wrote a suicide note, climbed into his silver Mazda and drove off a cliff, killing himself. He was grieving over his mother, who had died a year and a half before.

Mourning is simply an outward expression of an inward pain. Mourning and sorrow will flee, unless a person who is mourning picks up a spirit of grief, which leads to further loss and eventual destruction. Here is what the Word says about mourning:

> *They shall obtain gladness and joy; and sorrow and mourning shall flee away.*
>
> ISAIAH 51:11

*Thou hast turned for me my mourning into dancing: thou
hast put off my sackcloth, and girded me with gladness.*

PSALM 30:11

We need to understand there are different Greek and
Hebrew words for "grief." Jesus was grieved over the
hardness of people's hearts. (Mark 3:5.) The Holy Spirit
gets grieved over disobedience in the life of a believer.
(Eph. 4:30.) The apostle Paul was grieved in his spirit over
a demon-possessed girl's words and actions. (Acts 16:18.)
I'm not talking about that kind of grief. I am talking about
the *relentless* grief over a loss or perceived loss.

Even some preachers tell us the so-called grieving
process is good. As sincere as they are, it sounds to me as if
they received their "revelation" from a psychology book,
rather than from the Word of God. Perhaps they are just
using the word *grief* in the wrong context. I just know that
Jesus said, **Blessed are they that mourn.** (Matt. 5:4.) He
never said, "Blessed are they that live in grief." In fact, we
are told that Jesus actually bore our griefs and sorrows in
this Scripture:

Surely he hath borne our griefs, and carried our sorrows.

ISAIAH 53:4

When you face a loss, you can do one of two things. You
can go forward, or you can go backward. You can become
better, or you can become bitter. The outcome of your life
after facing a loss depends upon your decisions. If you
decide to allow the spirit (or attitude) of grief to stay with
you, your life will deteriorate and may even self-destruct.

I know the pain of saying good-bye to someone you love. It's awful. The pain is real. The lonely Christmases, the empty birthdays and weary holidays all serve as gruesome reminders that your loved one is gone. The feelings are real. The emotions are intense. But that doesn't mean they are true or dependable. Feelings and emotions are *not* dependable or accurate most of the time, but God's Word is.

Mourning is good because it will turn to joy. Mourning is healthy, because it will turn to dancing. Let me share with you the story of a real hero—a victorious overcomer. As a young pastor, Shorty, an eighty-five-year-old man, was a precious member of our congregation. I received a call when Shorty's wife of sixty years died suddenly. I drove over to Shorty's apartment in the city housing project. There he sat in his little living room with a silly smile on his face. It was almost as if he was envious that she'd gone to heaven first.

I tried to comfort him by saying, "Shorty, I'm so sorry you lost your precious wife."

"Oh, I didn't lose her. I know right where she's at!"

Of course, Shorty mourned for his wife. He missed her and was lonely for her at times. He had many blessed memories of their life and service for Christ together. But Shorty refused to allow the spirit of grief to rest upon him. He started working around the apartment building, planting flowers, mowing the lawn and cleaning things for people. He made himself so valuable to the complex that the city leaders lowered his rent because of all the work he was doing. He blessed all those elderly folks who lived in the building. He helped people who locked themselves out of their apartments, arranged Bible studies and stayed very active. Everybody else's rent was going up, but the city now paid Shorty to live in the complex because he had become so useful and productive.

Shorty mourned, but that mourning turned into dancing and joy because he refused to allow an attitude of grief to penetrate his heart. He rebounded from his loss and was more productive, more successful and more prosperous than ever before. He chose to rebound rather than rebel.

Mourning in a scriptural way will bring blessings and enlargement and set you in a wealthy place, as this Scripture says:

> *We went through fire and through water: but thou broughtest us out into a wealthy place.*

> PSALM 66:12

On our journey through life, sooner or later we all face the pain of a personal "Baca." The Valley of Baca was an actual place in biblical days known as the "Valley of Tears" or the "Valley of Weeping."

> *Blessed is the man whose strength is in thee; in whose heart are the ways of them. Who passing through the valley of Baca make it a well; the rain also filleth the pools. They go from strength to strength, every one of them in Zion appeareth before God.*

> PSALM 84:5-7

This valley has come to symbolize any tough or painful event that causes us emotional hurt. It is a place of seeming uncertainty and stress, but God gave promises for those who go *through* the Valley of Baca and resolve not to stop there. He promised that "Baca" will only be a temporary point in your journey through life and that you will be filled with an unlimited supply (rain for your pools) and will gain supernatural victorious power! All this is promised to those who mourn but refuse to slip into the attitude of grief.

I know you want to go forward and not backward. You want to become better, not bitter. You want to rebound, not rebel. Allow me to present you with seven simple keys for the kind of mourning that leads to joy, dancing and increase.

First, set a time limit for your mourning. Time does not heal anything. Five years after my dad died, I still was not healed from that trauma. Waiting around for time to heal your pain is fruitless. Jesus is the Healer. You must set a time limit on mourning if it is to turn to joy and dancing.

Time did not heal the pain for a man who lost his wife and two beautiful teenage daughters in a school bus accident caused by a drunk driver. His mind simply rehearsed how they burned to death in that fiery crash. He could find no peace or relief from the pain until he made a decision to set a time limit on his mourning. He set a date for it to be over, after which he refused to mourn. When he did this, God worked a miracle in his heart, restored his passion for life and gave him a beautiful new wife with whom to start a new life.

Second, pray in the Spirit. When you pray in the Spirit, you pray without human understanding and your spirit is energized and built up as He gives you heavenly understanding. Proverbs 3:5 says, **Trust in the Lord with all thine heart; and lean not unto thine own understanding.** When tragedy strikes, you don't understand; but during seasons of prayer, God just may reveal wonderful things to you about your loved one and show you important keys and principles to apply in your life.

Third, ask the Lord to give your loved one a message. Necromancy, the practice of talking to the dead, is forbidden in the Bible. Prayer to God, however, is not forbidden but encouraged. I remember standing at my father's grave for the first time fourteen years after his death. Standing there weeping, I looked up into the heavens and said, "Jesus, You are God. Will You please tell my dad that I love him—I really love him? Let him know that I'm a preacher now, if he doesn't already know. Tell him he'd be proud of me, like he was when I won the track meets in high school. Thank You, Lord." What a peace and amazing release enveloped me! Something happened that closed the book on all those guilt-ridden years of never telling my dad that I loved him.

Fourth, start praising God with reckless abandon. Lift your hands. Dance around your house shouting praises to God and watch how the garment of praise peels off that old rag of heaviness. (Isa. 61:3.)

Fifth, speak out loud to others of your intention to move ahead in God's will, regardless of this setback. The devil can make some pretty powerful arguments for your *right* to grieve. He will accuse you, tell you all the wrong things you did and use any other tool he can employ to get you into a position of perpetual grief. Only faith-filled words spoken from God's Word can clobber him and drive his thoughts far from your mind. Jesus used simple phrases from God's Word to overcome the devil. (Matt. 4:4-10.) Speak God's Word, God's will and your intentions of moving ahead.

Sixth, get busy again. Do whatever it is you are called to do. It's okay to take a short break, but there comes a time to get up and move on. Do what Shorty did, and reach out to others. Do what Harry and Cheryl have done, and keep right on ministering the Gospel.

Start moving ahead and verbalize to as many people as possible your full intentions of serving God all of your days, no matter what. It will not only bring you into a "wealthy place"; it will be a witness to others of your abiding faith in Jesus Christ. Those who allow their lives to stop because of the spirit of grief can never be a witness of Christ's amazing love and restoring power.

Seventh, make Jesus Christ Lord of your life, if you haven't already. Only He has the power to make all things new. God gave only one plan to make you fit for heaven, and that plan is a Man—Jesus Christ. It was He who took our infirmities and bore our sicknesses. (Matt. 8:17.) He bore our griefs and sorrows (Isa. 53:4), and He alone has the power to pull you through the "Valley of Tears" successfully. God has no "Plan B."

This is the starting point for turning mourning into joy and dancing. God is completely in love with you. Accept His love as a free gift from Him to you.

The choice to rebel or rebound belongs to each of us. We can go forward with our lives or backwards. Just the fact that you are reading this book tells me you are choosing to rebound, as Harry and Cheryl have done. I know you will see a bright, abundant future begin to unfold before your very eyes.

First the Test, Now the Trial

by Harry Salem

One of the key rules of warfare is to never turn your back on the enemy. Just because it appears the battle is over doesn't mean the danger is gone. Many a hunter has tracked a grizzly bear through the mountains and given up only to discover the bear has circled around and is, in fact, tracking him. Weather trackers also warn us not to be lulled into thinking a storm's fury has been spent just because the wind dies down and the sun comes back out. It may just be that the eye of the storm is passing over and the worst is yet to come. When heavy rain causes rivers to flood, the highest water may come days after the rain has stopped, because it takes time for the accumulation of water from the runoff to flow down. What I am saying here is this: Don't let your guard down just because a time of testing appears to have come to an end, because now comes the trial.

You will find that you are the most vulnerable after going through an intense testing, such as we did with Gabrielle. You're tired, weary and battle-worn. Cheryl shared with you in chapter 8 how the enemy deceived her into taking a reprieve from keeping herself built up in the Word and prayer and how later, with her own words, she made herself a target for the enemy. She was in a dangerous place.

Keep Your Guard Up

The enemy is always lurking around looking for an opportunity to take us out, as it says in this Scripture:

Be sober, be vigilant; because your adversary the devil walks about like a roaring lion, seeking whom he may devour. Resist him, steadfast in the faith, knowing that the same sufferings are experienced by your brotherhood in the world.

1 PETER 5:8 NKJV

We must be vigilant at all times, resist him, stand strong in our faith and never turn our backs. It is interesting to note that in ancient days warriors wore all their armor in front. Their backs were unprotected. Thus, a warrior was never to turn his back on the enemy. God's armor is the same. It protects us as we advance toward the enemy and resist him, but not if we turn our backs on him.

Gaining Greater Maturity

Those first few months after Gabrielle's home-going, we were numb with the pain of separation. We thought the battle was over and didn't realize we were just in the eye of the storm. Three months later, when Cheryl was diagnosed with colon cancer and taken into surgery, we knew our test was not over. We quickly regrouped for battle. We hadn't lost our faith because Gabrielle had chosen to go on ahead of us. Our faith was stronger than ever, and we trusted the Lord no matter what the outcome.

The good thing about a test is that it brings you the strength to go up to a higher level of faith. Without testing, you don't mature in your Christian walk. You would never move beyond where you were at the time of your salvation. It is simply a fact that if you walk with Jesus, you are going to be tested; and you'd better learn something along the way for the next time of testing, because there will *always* be a next time. It is better to pass the test the first time and not have to walk through the desert for forty years, as the children of Israel did. None of us want a twelve-day trip to last forty years.

We thought the battle was over and didn't realize we were just in the eye of the storm.

A trial is what you *do* with everything you've learned up till this point with your faith. It is like taking a driving test. You study and prepare for it in advance. Once you take the test and pass it, you are licensed to drive on the highway. If you then forget everything you've learned in preparing for the test, you are either going to have a wreck or get a ticket. You have to remember what you've learned and been prepared to do.

People who see you go through a test are going to be watching to see how you go through the trial. It is unbelievable what people will say. At Gabrielle's home-going celebration a man actually walked up to me and said, "Well, I guess you didn't have enough faith for your daughter's healing"! Cheryl had to restrain me. I was looking for a Holy Ghost flamethrower (my chosen physical weapon of battle)!

It is simply a fact that if you walk with Jesus, you are going to be tested; and you'd better learn something along the way for the next time of testing, because there will always be a next time.

We received thousands of letters and notes and a few were sprinkled with similar comments, such as "You just should have believed God and not used that medicine," or "There must have been something in your past or a curse on your life." Such people are trying to find an answer, when the problem is they have not learned how to balance their faith with trust. It is the skeptics who are going to stand back with their arms folded and say, "Okay, let's see how you make it through this trial."

See God's Word in Action

We don't have to answer the skeptics, and we won't be held in condemnation. We know *the* answer: Jesus restores! However, from the testing *and* the trial comes forth a testimony, which we hold in highest regard. It is by our

People who see you go through a testing are going to be watching to see how you go through the trial.

testimony that people see God's Word in action. By sharing with you some of the things we learned walking through our test and trial, we hope to prepare you for your own tests and trials and help ease your transition from preparation to action.

Restoration Begins at Home

Gabrielle's home-going was two days before Thanksgiving. That holiday was somewhat of a blur with a lot of people coming and going and mountains of food being brought to the house. We got through it, but I knew Christmas was going to be hard.

As a rule, Christmas was huge at our house, with lights, trees, packages, Christmas movies, carols and every family thing you could do. We would sit around the piano, and Cheryl would play while the children sang. We were always the first to buy a tree at the Christmas tree sales display. We put up the tree early so that on Thanksgiving Day everyone coming to our house for dinner or just to visit knew it was the beginning of the holiday season.

December was a celebration month at our house. As a family we decorated the tree and the house and put up the outdoor lights. They might not have been straight, but we were always amazed at the beauty even in the imperfect work. Cheryl never failed to come out and inspect our work putting up the outside lights, saying, "There's a bulb out..." (I fell off the roof twice.) In our neighborhood, most people pay to have their yards decorated professionally, but ours was an act of love.

This year was different. Right after Thanksgiving, we took the boys to Florida for some family time together. Then we flew to the West Coast. After returning home from California and ministering on TBN, Benny Hinn's program and other national programs, I was thinking as we drove home from the airport, about ten days before Christmas, *We don't have a tree; we don't have any lights up, and we haven't bought one gift. The boys will be so disappointed.*

Was I in for a surprise! When we drove up to our house, it was just aglow with thousands of Christmas lights. The people at Rhema Church had come out and professionally decorated the entire house. It was so beautiful. The boys were just shocked. We stopped out in front and just stared.

Then when we went inside, to our amazement, we found that my mom and some of her friends, my sisters and a dear friend named Pam had decorated the inside. All that was left for us to do was put up a tree. We had to find the right one the next day. We were being restored.

We have a fake tree for the living room that the boys call "the girls' tree," because it has angels and frilly stuff on it. But the "boys' tree," a real tree, is always in the family room.

We went out the next night to get a Christmas tree, only to discover that the three places we normally went were all out of trees. Roman began to cry, "We're not going to have a Christmas tree. Santa's going to forget us…." We drove up to another place, and all they had left were huge tall trees that would fit only inside a mall. We found one that had a nice shape to it, and I said, "That's it. We're taking it. Shove it in the van." I paid $100 for that tree—the most I've ever paid for a Christmas tree in my life. Then I had to cut it almost in two to fit it in the house.

I was determined to make it the best Christmas possible for our family. The boys had been through so much, and I probably went overboard with presents and special plans. It was difficult to see only two stocking hanging on the mantle.

A Turning Point

With Christmas approaching Cheryl was really struggling to put up a good front for the boys, but let me share how the Lord intervened. What we learned from this was a turning point in our family's healing process.

Cheryl never holds back from the Lord exactly how she feels. She says we might as well be honest with Him because He knows us better than we know ourselves anyway. She was feeling really down about Christmas without Gabrielle, and she said, "Oh, Lord, I don't know how I'm going to get through this season and certainly not Christmas Day." She poured out her heart about how hard it was going to be.

The Lord said, *Cheryl, if you focus on what you* don't *have, you will lose what you* do *have!* Then He added, *And don't you dare ruin My birthday!*

These words changed Cheryl's whole perspective. She realized she did not want to risk losing our wonderful boys, our marriage and ministry by focusing on something she could not change. When she shared with the family what the Lord had said to her, our son Roman with his young boy's godly wisdom said, "This is the day the Lord has made. He said we should rejoice and be glad in it!" That is what the Lord wants us to understand. No matter what we are going through or how hard it is, every day is His day and He wants us to rejoice and be glad in it. Christmas was a good day, and Cheryl was able to get through it without any tears.

Let's read what the apostle Paul wrote about this:

Not that I am implying that I was in any personal want, for I have learned how to be content (satisfied to the point where I am not disturbed or disquieted) in whatever state I am. I know how to be abased and live humbly in straitened circumstances, and I know also how to enjoy plenty and live in abundance. I have learned in any and all circumstances the secret of facing every situation, whether well-fed or going hungry, having a sufficiency and enough to spare or going without and being in want. I have strength for all things in Christ Who empowers me

[I am ready for anything and equal to anything through Him Who infuses inner strength into me; I am self-sufficient in Christ's sufficiency].

PHILIPPIANS 4:11-13 AMP

In a nutshell, that is how we can get through anything. When we focus on drawing our strength from Christ, who is in us, we are ready for and equal to whatever comes our way—no matter how good or bad it is.

The Attack on the Family

A Christian attorney who practices family law and specializes in helping families with physically or mentally challenged children says she sees too many families torn apart by the stress of raising such a child. A nurse who works in a neonatal unit shared that when a newborn is diagnosed with severe physical or mental challenges, staff members often comment that another divorce is in the making. The enemy attacks when we are at our weakest and under the heaviest stress, and that is when we must be vigilant.

When we focus on drawing our strength from Christ, who is in us, we are ready for and equal to whatever comes our way—no matter how good or bad it is.

Dispelling the Myth

Many people have told us that the divorce rate is unusually high for couples who experience the death of a child. Some say it is as high as 80 to 90 percent. We did some research and discovered this is a myth. Bereaved couples must understand the importance of communication and recognize that each family member will grieve differently, but they shouldn't be placed under the added burden of an expectation that their marriage is doomed.

Bereaved couples must understand the importance of communication and recognize that each family member will grieve differently, but they shouldn't be placed under the added burden of an expectation that their marriage is doomed.

Government statistics estimate that each year 228,000 children and young adults die in the United States. This statistic does not include miscarriages, stillbirths or deaths of older adults (age 40+) whose parents survive them.[1]

The following information was taken from a survey of bereaved parents conducted by NFO Research, Inc., on behalf of The Compassionate Friends, Inc., in June 1999. The Compassionate Friends (TCF) is an organization that provides support and understanding to families following the death of a child, regardless of the age of the child or the cause of death.

An initial survey questionnaire was sent to a random sampling of 20,000 adults taken from NFO's national panel of 250,000 households. A total of 14,852 surveys were returned. From nearly 3000 bereaved parents' names obtained in the initial survey, a random sample of 290 men and 304 women was contacted by telephone in February 1999. Here are some important statistics from the survey:

- 19 percent of the adult population has experienced the death of a child and 22 percent the death of a sibling; 36 percent of the adult population has suffered the death of a child, sibling or both a child and a sibling.

- Miscarriage is the most prevalent cause of death (43 percent), followed by illness (27 percent), accident (13 percent), and stillbirth (11 percent). The majority of deaths by illness occur in children over age 21, while accidents are most likely in the teen/adult years.

- Overall, 72 percent of parents who were married at the time of their child's death are still married to the same person. The remaining 28 percent of marriages include 16 percent in which one spouse had died, and only 12 percent of marriages that ended in divorce. Furthermore, even among the 12 percent of parents whose marriages ended in divorce, only one out of four of them felt that the impact of the death of their child contributed to their divorce.[2]

We realize this is only one study, and due to the sample composition may understate the percentage of divorces impacted by the death of a child; but it is sufficient evidence to indicate the divorce rate is *significantly* lower in the general population than often stated. We must be vigilant to protect our families from the threat of divorce and division.

Keep the Right Attitude

Through this test we learned how to be content in whatever state we are in by keeping our attitudes right and staying focused on what we *do* have. We don't try to justify why it happened. We aren't like the stock market, up one day and down the next. We have learned to rejoice in all situations and keep our focus on Jesus.

People frequently say to us, "We don't know how you're getting through it." We have no choice. Gabrielle didn't quit, and we won't either! Besides, our foundation is based on the Word, not the world. We concentrate on having higher thoughts, eternal thoughts, rather than earthly thoughts. Yes, it's tough. Yes, we get sad. Yes, we miss her. There are some restaurants we can't eat in and some movies

We have learned to rejoice in all situations and to keep our focus on Jesus.

and children's programs we can't watch and some books we can't read. We can't walk down the Barbie aisle in a toy store.

No Camping Allowed

The key is moving *through* the mourning and the grief and the separation. God doesn't want us to stay there. He wants us to go *through* the valley of the shadow of death to the other side. He wants us to go *through* the desert. That doesn't mean bringing along your pup tent and your underwear and toothbrush to set up housekeeping. Sometimes people get comfortable in the midst of their grief and just decide to stay there. Cheryl says, "Run like your pants are on fire. This is no time for dilly dallying." Just keep moving, one step at a time, one day at a time, and you'll get to the other side.

Learning To Learn

Another important key is to keep learning in the midst of the test so you can apply what you learn to the trial that comes next. I'll never forget what T.L. Osborn, a great man of God, said when I asked him how he was doing after his precious wife, Daisy, went home to be with the Lord. He said, "I'm learning."

"What are you learning?"

"I'm learning to learn."

"What do you mean 'learning to learn'?"

"I'm learning to learn how to get through each day without Daisy."

At eighty-plus years of age, he is still learning.

The apostle Paul said in the Scripture we read from Philippians 4:12-13 AMP that he had learned the secret of facing every situation. The secret is that we have strength for all things through Christ who empowers us. The word *empower* is a verb that requires action. Christ gives you the power to do whatever it takes to get *through* every situation, no matter how difficult it might be.

Let's suppose you are a highly qualified carpenter and have all the tools needed to perform your trade. I hire you to build a new porch and tell you to be on the job Monday morning at 9:00 A.M. If you show up with your tools but just sit and do nothing with them, I'm going to fire you. That is the way most of us use the strength God has given us. We have it, but we don't *do* anything with it.

Don't Get Weary

We know what it means to get weary in well doing. We did three blood draws on Gabrielle each week, which meant three trips, usually driving the big motor coach, to a hospital or laboratory to get it processed. Cheryl had to work three hours every morning with Gabrielle to prepare and administer her medicine and therapy. It took her another three hours to get her settled down for the night.

Then there were numerous trips to the potty during the night. Gabrielle's weight went from thirty-seven pounds up to ninety-seven pounds, which meant we had to carry her in and out of the motor coach and lift her in and out of the stroller.

What did we learn through all of this? This wasn't the time to stop, to give up or to feel sorry for ourselves. We stayed out on the road ministering as much as possible. We were holding on for and with Gabrielle. If she could do it, we could do it. When we were weary and tired, God showed up every time. In our weakness, He was strong.

Rejoice in the Lord

Have you ever gone to church and been so tired you didn't want to participate in anything, especially praise and worship? Then the music started and even though you didn't feel like singing, you did it anyway. You didn't want to lift your hands, but you lifted them anyway. You didn't want to clap, but you clapped anyway. You didn't feel like dancing, but your feet just started moving to the rhythm. Suddenly you were feeling better and even enjoying it. You may not have realized it, but you had just been re-infused with the power of the Holy Ghost. It's like you'd just received a Holy Ghost transfusion right into your spirit man. You didn't really do anything to earn it. You just showed up, made your flesh come under submission and your spirit man was infused.

At Gabrielle's home-going celebration Kenneth Copeland said, "God will re-joy you." That is something you must *choose* to let Him do. That means He again fills you up with joy, and the best place to receive that is in His house worshipping with other believers. You can do it at home, but the easiest way to get your tank refilled is when you are with other believers entering into His presence together. The anointing is strongest in a multitude of worshipers. In the presence of such anointing you will forget about all problems, pain and worry.

Perfecting Praise

Never underestimate the power of praise and worship. In our book *An Angel's Touch*, Cheryl shares how she would see angels appear at different times during services. At one service in New Orleans an angel spoke to her and said,

> *You have often wondered why we appear at different times in the service. We are released to come in when the praise becomes pure. Not when you think it's pure, but when God knows it is pure by the hearts of the people. Then we are allowed to come in and do our jobs.*[3]

When the praise of our hearts becomes pure before God, the angels come on the scene and bring many gifts, such as miracles, restoration, a breakthrough, healing and so forth.

From another excerpt of this same book, I want to share how the transfer takes place from the supernatural to the natural.

I sat in astonishment and awe as person after person was touched by an angel with the miracle God had sent for each one. If I live to be 200 years old, I'll never forget how I felt watching that miraculous interchange of faith and miracles! Faith literally took on the form of a substance in the supernatural realm. As faith was released to God, a type of exchange occurred. Faith was released, and a miracle was received. That night I watched in wonder as the angels brought God's healing gifts and miracles to His people.[4]

It is when we are at our weakest and submit ourselves to the Lord in complete humility that our praise becomes pure. It is an attitude of the heart. That is when His miracles come to us.

Only a month or two after Gabrielle's diagnosis, someone sent us the song "This Test is Your Storm." We have claimed it as our own. Let these words minister to your spirit as they do to ours every time Cheryl sings them:

I have listened to you; I've heard your requests.
I've come to tell you that it's only a test.
Just hold on, through your storm. Be strong.
Just hold on. This test is your storm, but it won't
　　be long.
Just hold on.
So your daughter won't hear you, son could care less.
Seems they've done all to hurt you, but it's only a test.
Just hold on through your storm. Be strong, and
　　hold on.
This test is your storm, but it won't be long. Go
　　through. Hold on.

Don't you know that the darkest time in your life is just
  before the break of dawn?
The promise of "Your Battles, I will fight" if you just
  hold on.

Your tears have been plenty in the still of the night.
You've prayed; now you're empty, just to reap, just
  to fight.
Just hold on, through your storm. Be strong and
  hold on.
This test is your storm, but it won't be long. Go
  through. Hold on.

You say you've been wounded, you've given your best,
You've been misunderstood; but it's only a test.
This test is your storm, but it won't be long. Go
  through. Hold on.

God said, "I AM ABLE to deliver you. Hold on. Hold on."
He said, "I AM ABLE. I can deliver you. Hold on.
  Hold on."
He said, "I can help you with My outstretched hand.
  Hold on. Hold on. Hold on."
He said, "I AM ABLE. I can heal you. Hold on. Hold on.
  Hold on."
"By My stripes, you are healed. Hold on. Hold on.
  Hold on."

Don't you ever quit. Don't give in. Hold on, my
  brother.
Don't give in, my sister. Hold on. Hold on.
We've gotta hold on. Don't ever give in.
We've gotta hold on.

"I can see you through each and every trial."
God will see you through.[5]

So, if you are in the midst of a test or a trial and feel like you can't go on, don't give up—just hold on. Your hope is not in the circumstances. Your hope is in the Lord. Keep your focus on the need meeter—Jesus. He holds the key to making it *through* to the other side. He has empowered you to make it. No matter what storm you are going through, God is with you. He has not left you or forsaken you. Just hold on. Let Him "re-joy" you, and keep learning to learn because the Son will shine in the morning.

Keep your focus on the need meeter—Jesus. He holds the key to making it through to the other side.

RE-Joice in the Lord!

by Kenneth Copeland

A s people who live and walk by faith, we are a blessed people; but that also makes us a targeted people. We are the most dangerous generation Satan has ever come up against. In 6000 years he has never faced this many people on this planet at the same time who believe in God. On top of that, he is faced with the Church *and* Israel on the earth at the same time. So he's divided on two fronts, and he has a lot of problems. I intend to continue to be one of them, and I know you do, too. We are a people of faith.

Some months ago, the Lord showed me that there are things arrayed against us that we don't know anything about. There is far more arrayed against us than we really have any concept of unless God opens our eyes to it—and occasionally He does—so we can charge the wall and stop certain things.

As a young boy, my uncle (my mother's brother) gave his life for this country in Europe during World War II. I remember my grandmother's terrible cries as over and over and over she screamed, "Why? Oh why? Oh why?" Even as a little boy, I was really affected. I was marked by that experience with death, and over the years I asked a lot of questions about it.

My grandmother's generation did not have the spiritual knowledge and the kind of faith that you and I walk in and know. They were wonderful people and loved God but in a much smaller framework than what you and I are now blessed with in our generation.

Today I can explain the "why?" A demon-possessed madman by the name of Adolph Hitler, under the influence of Satan, started a war. He had to be stopped, and that war had to be finished. In every war men die. My uncle, along with hundreds of thousands of men and women, laid down his life so that we might live in freedom.

The designer and director of the persecution of God's people through Adolph Hitler is the same one who designed brain tumors. The same wicked, evil enemy who designed that terrible war is the designer of every battle in which you and I are involved in this world today.

Medical technology never, ever will be at a place where we can relax and depend on it for all of our medical needs. It can never come to that place because of the spiritual roots in sickness and disease. There are areas that the natural world can't even contact. You just can't get there through natural technology. You have to get there with spiritual technology. So there are still a lot of questions for which we don't have answers, because our spiritual technology is not at that level. It is not at the level that we all wish and believe for it to be as we grow and mature in the Lord.

Rather than asking, "God, why?" and "How did You let this happen?" our question should be "God, how did I, through my lack of spiritual knowledge, allow this to progress?" Now, hear what I am saying. The key is not to ask it in condemnation but to ask it *in faith.* (I want you to know I am being obedient to what the Lord told me to write. I am not saying the Salem family needs to ask this question. They had the faith and never gave up. This word is for the body of Christ at this hour.)

This is the time in God's plan for us to conscientiously question the Word of God and question ourselves so we can continue to learn and develop and continue to believe God and stretch as we have never stretched before. Through prayer we have gained some spiritual ground in this generation. Hundreds of years before us, people prayed and hoped one day to see into what you and I are ministering in and walking in on a daily basis.

The spirit of grief is one of the most dangerous and one of the most committed evil workings of Satan with which everyone comes into contact. This is one area in which God's people need to improve their spiritual knowledge and technology. The thing that amazes me is that some of God's people know Satan **cometh but to kill and to steal and to destroy** (John 10:10), and yet they have a tendency to blame God more than they blame the devil.

I blame the devil for everything I can find to blame him for, and I love to do it. I blame him for everything from fleas to the dogs that carry them. I do despise him. The only thing I despise worse than him is his work.

Our thinking has to remain focused and concentrated on the Word of God in order to bridge the gap in the areas that we don't understand. In seeking God and pressing in to the things of God during the loss of one of our most precious family members—my mother—we gained the spiritual technology that we later used when one of Kellie's children almost died of Nigerian Meningitis. We were able to take that knowledge and press through that thing and keep the devil from stealing another one.

Do you remember when Jesus ministered to the rich young ruler? Let's read this account in the Scripture:

> *Now as He was going out on the road, one came running, knelt before Him, and asked Him, "Good Teacher, what shall I do that I may inherit eternal life?"*
>
> *So Jesus said to him, "Why do you call Me good? No one is good but One, that is, God. You know the commandments: 'Do not commit adultery,' 'Do not murder,' 'Do not steal,' 'Do not bear false witness,' 'Do not defraud,' 'Honor your father and your mother.'"*
>
> *And he answered and said to Him, "Teacher, all these I have kept from my youth."*
>
> *Then Jesus, looking at him, loved him, and said to him, "One thing you lack: Go your way, sell whatever you have and give*

to the poor, and you will have treasure in heaven; and come, take up the cross, and follow Me."

But he was sad at this word, and went away sorrowful, for he had great possessions.

MARK 10:17-22 NKJV

Now, there's the ministry of the spirit of grief: sadness or sorrow and separation from the One who has the right answer. The young man walked away because of a sense of loss or sorrow.

This is the area of spiritual technology in which the Lord instructed me when my mother went home to be with Him. They told me she wasn't going to live but thirty-six hours. The Lord helped me in the middle of that by ministering to her in a totally different avenue than what I'd expected. Her life was sustained for a nine-month period of time.

During that time, the Lord prepared me and I learned something from the Word of God that all of us need at one time or another. Jesus bore our grief and carried our sorrow. Our spiritual assignment on this earth, our job in the suffering that we face on this earth as born-again, spiritually oriented people of God is to resist with all our hearts, all our minds, all our bodies and all our possessions, everything that He bore for us on that cross.

He bore our sin, so we are to resist sin. He bore our sickness, so we are to resist sickness. Praise God, if there ever was an example of that, it is the Salem family and little Gabrielle. They resisted this thing. I thank God for their testimony of standing against what Jesus bore for us on the cross.

Now, this is the part that the Lord directly began to develop in me during the last nine months of my mother's life in 1988 and that has totally reoriented my life since then. When we resist what Jesus bore for us on the cross, and we resist it by faith, by the Word, by revelation from God until we press all the way *through* to the end to our victory in Christ Jesus, on the other end of that resistance is the key, the source of our strength: joy. You don't recognize it if you're not aware of it. And this was an area of truth that God really helped me in where my mother was concerned and has helped me in other areas of my life since. It has been so valuable to me.

My mother went home to be with the Lord right in the middle of the Fort Worth Believer's Convention. Somebody said, "Well, you're not going to preach the service tonight, are you?" I said, "Well the quickest way I know to raise mother from the dead would be for me not to preach a service on account of her going to heaven. She would rise up and spank me again if she found out I did something like that."

I already was armed with this truth. When we begin to really press in to the Word of God, we're putting pressure against what Jesus bore for us on the cross. In this case, it was sorrow and grief. When we begin to press, the force that comes up to sustain us is the joy of the Lord. I didn't recognize it for what it actually was until the Lord pointed it out to me.

Now, joy doesn't appear as you and I think it should. We recognize joy when the bubbly, jumping up and down and so forth comes, and that's coming. That's the manifestation of the victory of this thing.

But the joy of the Lord, which is our strength, is what comes up inside us and gives us a deeper resolve in the faith of what we are pressing against. And when you press in and just absolutely refuse to quit or to be defeated, and continue pressing no matter what happens, the joy of the Lord is there. That's your strength, and if you press *through* to that joy, then the jumping up and down and bubbly kind of joy does come. It is inevitable. Once you learn how to do that, you'll never have that kind of fight with it again. It's the most marvelous thing. The general body of Christ knows absolutely nothing of it. It has to become a way of life.

The final thing that the Lord wanted me to say is this. The true meaning of the word *rejoice* is to "re-joy yourselves." Again, I say, "re-joy yourselves." "Re-joice!" "Re-joice in the name of Jesus!" Take a stand against the spirit of death, the spirit of grief and anything else the devil would attempt to sow into your life. Resist everything Jesus bore for you on the cross and stand strong in the name of Jesus, because the joy of the Lord is your strength!

A Time To Shout, "Restore!"

by Cheryl Salem

Restoration is a process. It doesn't happen overnight. It comes one step at a time. We hated the test we had to go through, but our testimony has been perfected in the trial. The devil causes bad things to happen, but God gets all the glory through our testimony. It is by our testimony that we are making the devil pay for what he has done. We didn't go through all that we did for any personal want or gain, and neither did Gabrielle. We did it for what others can gain out of it for the ministry of the gospel. We have to take this message of restoration and eternal life to the world, because Gabrielle gave her life for it!

Four days before Gabrielle went home to be with the Lord, Dr. Oral Roberts came to our home. As he talked with us, the Spirit of the Lord came upon him, and he began to prophesy. He said we were like Shadrach, Meshach and Abednego in the fiery furnace, and when we came out of the fire we wouldn't even smell of smoke. (See Dan. 3.) That word was confirmation, because the Lord had spoken those same words to me at the very beginning of our test. When the doctors first spoke the evil report of the diagnosis, the Lord said we wouldn't smell of smoke and

It is by our testimony that we are making the devil pay for what he has done.

neither would Gabrielle. We held on to those words as our promise of total and complete restoration. It *is* happening. Not the way we expected, but it is happening.

Restoration: Better Than Before

Harry's father was a car dealer. As a little boy, Harry often went with his father to the dealership. He loved to watch the mechanics restore old cars. To do it properly they had to take the car completely apart. Sometimes the bolts were really rusty, and the men bloodied their knuckles and got their hands soiled and dirty in the process. They laid out all the parts on the floor, sanded them all down, put primer on each part and began to put the car back together again. When the restoration process was complete, that automobile was better than the day it was built in the factory. It was better for two reasons: (1) There was more tender, loving care put into the workmanship, and (2) they did it with their own hands.

Restored by the Hands of Jesus

Jesus is using His hands to restore our family, and He will use His hands to restore you with tender loving care.

There is an appointed time to shout for restoration and an appointed time for your victory.

We have taken the "U" out of mourning and are moving forward to live out Gabrielle's and our testimonies so others may live. We made a choice to go on *through* the valley of the shadow of death, *through* the test of Gabrielle's illness and then my surgery. We have stepped into a new level of faith *and* trust, and we are moving

onward and upward to take this message of restoration to God's people.

An Appointed Time

The people of God need restoration in their families, marriages, finances, health, emotions and every area of life. What the Lord showed me is that there is an appointed time to shout for restoration and an appointed time for your victory. The Scripture He gave me came from the story of Jericho. This is what it says:

> *When they make a long blast with the ram's horn and you hear the sound of the trumpet, all the people shall shout with a great shout; and the wall of the enclosure shall fall down in its place and the people shall go up [over it], every man straight before him.*
>
> *But Joshua commanded the people, You shall not shout or let your voice be heard, nor shall any word proceed out of your mouth until the day I tell you to shout. Then you shall shout!*

JOSHUA 6:5,10 AMP

It wasn't walking around the city of Jericho, being in agreement about what they were doing or blowing the trumpet that brought the walls down. It was the obedient act of shouting at God's appointed time that brought the walls down. There is victory in your mouth. It's not in your feet or in your hands; it's in your mouth. Your mouth is a tool to hook the supernatural and drag it into the natural. There is restoration in your mouth. Are you ready to shout, "Restore!"? Are you willing to be a fool for Christ and shout, "Restore! Restore!"?

There is victory in your mouth.

Victory Is in Your Mouth

You have to make up your mind that you are going to get out of captivity and that there is an appointed time for you to find your voice of triumph. We found ours at an appointed time. For me it was actually six months before Gabrielle became sick. The Lord led me to this Scripture:

> But this is a people robbed and plundered; all of them are snared in holes, and they are hidden in prison houses; they are for prey, and no one delivers; for plunder, and no one says, "Restore!" Who among you will give ear to this? Who will listen and hear for the time to come?
>
> ISAIAH 42:22,23 NKJV

I began to shout, "Restore!" over and over as I sat in my rocking chair praying in the morning. I didn't know for whom I was crying out, but I knew someone had to shout it out. I began to shout it out in the car driving down the road or in the bathroom putting on my makeup. I did that for months, and when Gabrielle got sick, I continued saying, "Father, I shout, *Restore for Your people! Restore for our family.*"

We received confirmation of this revelation the night Lindsay called us at two o'clock in the morning shouting "Wahoo!" The Lord had given her this same Scripture. Whether we shout, "Restore!" or "Wahoo!" it means the same thing: "God is able!" What was most important about all this was that the Lord had me shouting, "Restore!" *before* the crisis had hit. I had good seed in the ground, so the harvest was there when it was needed.

Job's Eternal Heritage

There is probably no greater example of restoration in the Scriptures than the restoration of Job. Let's read a key portion of this story:

> And the Lord turned the captivity of Job and restored his fortunes, when he prayed for his friends; also the Lord gave Job twice as much as he had before. Then there came to him all his brothers and sisters and all who had known him before, and they ate bread with him in his house; and they sympathized with him and comforted him over all the [distressing] calamities that the Lord had brought upon him. Every man also gave him a piece of money, and every man an earring of gold.
>
> And the Lord blessed the latter days of Job more than his beginning; for he had 14,000 sheep, 6,000 camels, 1,000 yoke of oxen, and 1,000 female donkeys.
>
> He had also seven sons and three daughters.
>
> JOB 42:10-13 AMP

When you compare what Job had at the beginning with what he had at the end, you will see that everything doubled. However, you may also note that he had seven sons and three daughters in the beginning *and* at the end. I noticed this same thing and said, "Lord, You doubled everything Job had in the beginning and blessed his later days; but when it came to the children, he had seven sons and three daughters in the beginning and seven sons and

189

three daughters at the end. Why didn't you double the number of his children?"

I did.

"But Lord, I'm looking right at it in the Word, and it says he had seven sons and three daughters in the beginning and the same number at the end."

I doubled the children. You think too earthly. You're going to have to learn if you walk with Me to think as I think, to move as I move and to do what I do.

"What are you saying, Lord?"

You call death life, and you call life death. When My people pass from here to eternity, you call that death, when it's the first time they have ever really lived. You speak of life and wanting My people to live longer on the earth, when that is as close to death as they will ever come. You have things backward. The second you accept Jesus as Lord and Savior of your life, you are born again. That is life—eternal life. You don't die and then pass into eternal life. The moment you are born again in Christ you have eternal life, and it is for eternity. You live forever.

"But I still don't understand about the seven sons and three daughters."

Look at it eternally. Job didn't lose his first seven sons and daughters, as he lost his camels, sheep and donkeys, because his children are eternal. Their earthly bodies died, but their spirits live on forever. When you look at what is on this earth, it is miniscule in comparison to eternity. Yet, you put so much emphasis on this little bit of life that you have here on this earth.

Now look at it as I do. I did double Job's children. For eternity, he will have fourteen sons and six daughters. You have to think as I think, move as I move, talk as I talk and walk as I walk.

I began to understand the revelation of what God was saying. He wants us to be heavenly minded. I used to say, "I'm so heavenly minded that I'm no earthly good." The Lord spoke to me one day and said, *I want you to be so heavenly minded that you are some earthly good.* I realized He is trying to get us to focus on eternity and live our lives with an eternal focus rather than focusing on the here and now.

We Have a Better Covenant

With all that we went through with Gabrielle and then with my surgery, people came up to Harry and said, "How much more can your family take? How much more can you withstand? You know, you are just like Job." He got in the Word and read Job and then read it again. From then on, when people said that to him, he stopped them immediately and said, "Hold it. Don't compare me to Job. Don't speak that over me. You don't know what kind of covenant Job had with God. I have a new covenant with God based on the blood Jesus shed for us. God didn't put this on us."

We have a better covenant than what Job had. What Job had at the end was good, but what we have is better than that.

Put a Demand on the Enemy

Did you know the devil doesn't mess with his own people? He hates God's people and tries to make their lives miserable, just as he did with Job, because he knows he can't get their souls back. The devil does everything he can to plunder and steal from God's people to keep them from fulfilling their destinies in Christ. It is up to you to put a demand on the devil to make him pay for everything he does to you. The Word tells us how to overcome the devil and all his wickedness:

It is up to you to put a demand on the devil to make him pay for everything he does to you.

And they overcame him by the blood of the Lamb and by the word of their testimony, and they did not love their lives to the death.

REVELATION 12:11 NKJV

Satan is a defeated foe. Jesus defeated him at Calvary 2000 years ago. All we are doing is enforcing his defeat with the weapons Jesus has given us: the blood of Jesus and the word of our testimony. Now can you see how important a testimony tried in the fire is?

I'm telling you, if no one else will shout, "Restore!" I'm going to shout it. If no one else will do it, I will be the one to stand up for the body of Christ and shout, "Restore!" I am demanding restoration because we have a right to it. God has promised it to us, and we need to learn to shout, "Restore!" into the heavens. It is the word of our testimony!

Restoration, Not Replacement

A man suffering from liver cancer doesn't need a new liver; he needs his own restored. He needs someone to begin to shout, "Restore!" for him. If your family is torn apart and scattered, you don't need a new family; you need the one you have restored. If your spouse doesn't act the way you want, you don't need a different spouse; you need the one you have restored. We live in a "disposable" society, and we need to get rid of that "throw away" mentality. Restoration is what is needed, not replacement. It is time to start shouting, "Restore!"

We live in a "disposable" society, and we need to get rid of that "throw away" mentality. Restoration is what is needed, not replacement.

Restoration takes time, and sometimes you get your knuckles bloodied in the process. However, if you will persevere and press on *through*, what is restored to you will be better than it was in the beginning. Why? It is better because you *did* something about it. You didn't just shout once; you shouted over and over until the supernatural became the natural, until the seen was swallowed up by the unseen. Now is your appointed time to shout, "Restore!" "Restore!" "Restore!"

Heaven's Viewpoint

by Billy Joe Daugherty

Our first encounter with Cheryl was some nineteen years ago when, after being crowned Miss America, she came to our city and sang and ministered at Victory Christian Center. Four years later, while co-hosting the Richard Roberts' Show, I met her again when she came to sing on the show. It was there that Harry and Cheryl met, and soon after they were married. Harry was working with the Roberts' ministries and ORU. Then along came Harry III, Roman and finally, their little sweetie, the beauty queen—Gabrielle. She was a joy in every way you can think—one who has touched the hearts of people all across America.

As Sharon and I, along with others, knelt at Gabrielle's bedside, we felt the mighty strength and power of God in a family that stood strong in their faith and believed God. We watched them walk through it all—even in the early morning when Gabrielle graduated to heaven.

When we think back of Gabrielle—or Gabs, or Sissy, as she was known by those closest to her—we think of someone who loved riding her bike, skateboarding, swimming, playing games and with her dolls. But most of all she loved to sing. In fact, it's reported that when she was born, she was more comfortable with a microphone than she was with a bottle! At a moment's notice, she was ready to sing her favorite songs—"Old Enough To Praise the Lord" and "Shout to the Lord."

A lot of people have been joined together because of Gabrielle. One letter that came from a Catholic bishop said, "This little girl is breaking down denominational walls as people have touched the heart of God and prayed and joined with this family."

Gabrielle was innocence, sweetness, purity and pure joy in the Holy Ghost, but she was also a trooper. In 1998 Salem Family Ministries preached and ministered in 260 services, and she sang in all of them. In 1999 she sang and ministered in 100 services. She would carry her IV backpack, which weighed 25 percent of her body weight, right up on stage and sing. She loved to sing duets with Mama. The Holy Spirit in her was able to move and reach out and touch people of every age, every denomination all across our land. The power of God moved through her in a very special way.

On November 23, 1999, her little spirit slipped out of her body, and she now has a new and glorified body. According to 2 Corinthians 5:1, it is a body not made with hands; it is eternal in the heavens. We also know that to be absent from the body is to be present with the Lord, and we must understand that from heaven's viewpoint, that moment of transition is glorious. The Bible says that moment is precious in the sight of the Lord. (Ps. 116:15.)

Gabrielle triumphed because of her faith in Jesus Christ. It is a no-lose, a win-win, position all the time. Think of these words from Scripture: **O Death, where is thy sting? O grave, where is thy victory? The sting of death is sin; and the strength of sin is the law. But thanks be to God, which giveth us the victory through our Lord Jesus Christ** (1 Cor. 15:55-57). He took our sin— the sting of it, the penalty of it. He was crucified and buried. Then on the third day God raised Jesus from the dead. And that same Spirit that raised Jesus from the dead was the Spirit inside Gabrielle.

So today she who believed in Jesus Christ is happy. She's alive. And right now she is singing in heaven. Jesus said, **I am the resurrection and the life. He who believes in Me, though he may die, he shall live. And whoever lives and believes in Me shall never die** (John 11:25,26 NKJV). That's why this family has chosen to celebrate Gabrielle's life, focusing on the resurrection, focusing on all the good things that have happened because of what Jesus did in her life and focusing on all the good things that He's doing right now in and through her. They are in continual celebration because they see from heaven's viewpoint. Gabrielle is rejoicing in heaven.

Nothing Is Too Much or Too Little

by Harry Salem

We weren't meant to make it through the tests and trials of life alone. Even the Lone Ranger had Tonto! We need others to stand in the gap for us, because isolation is one of the first steps to devastation. When we run out of strength, God sends people to hold up our arms and infuse us with more strength to keep fighting. One of the ways restoration comes is through the love and support of family and friends.

Our family could not have walked through all we have faced in the past two years without the people who came alongside us. Local churches in Tulsa reached out in many ways, sending meals every day for months before and after Gabrielle's home-going, holding prayer vigils, sending toys, dolls and cards, and financial gifts that enabled us to pay over $200,000 in medical bills. People all over the world were praying and fasting. Many came to our home and did

We need others to stand in the gap for us, because isolation is one of the first steps to devastation.

whatever they could to encourage and support us. I can't name everyone who helped, but I will share some of the things that brought restoration in the midst of our storm. This is an important part of our testimony, as it can be for yours.

A Knock on the Door

I remember one night in particular when Gabrielle's kidneys had shut down. The doctor said that if we didn't get them started again, we would have to take her into the hospital for dialysis. We had promised we would not take her to the hospital. At ten o'clock that night there was a knock on the door. I opened the door, and there stood Billy Joe and Sharon Daugherty in their nightclothes. That's a sight: wing-tipped shoes and pajamas! But it was a welcome sight.

Billy Joe said, "We were lying in bed praying for you and the Lord said to come. What's going on?" They lay on the floor at the foot of Gabrielle's bed for two hours and prayed.

I heard another knock on the door, and when I opened the door, it was Terry Law. He had just gotten off an airplane from China. He said, "While I was sitting on the airplane, the Lord said I was to come directly to your house. What is going on?" He sat in the rocking chair and prayed for the next two hours.

Another knock comes on the door. This time it was Eastman Curtis. He said, "I've been driving around your neighborhood praying. What's going on?" He came in and joined the prayer warriors: our attorney, my sister and others, besides those already mentioned.

Within two hours Gabrielle's kidneys began to function normally. God knew we needed more prayer support and the love of friends to carry us through the crisis. This sort of thing happened over and over throughout Gabrielle's illness. People came at just the right time.

God's Messengers

God knew exactly whom to send for each family member. My sister Stephanie came and spent the night almost every night; she was there for the boys. My mom traveled with us as often as possible, and she was there on the road and at home to help look after the boys and do whatever we needed. Cheryl's mom and step-dad drove from Mississippi once a month to be with us and to help any way they could. People came and took the boys out to a movie to give them something to do outside of the house. One night a lady from our church came and brought two frozen pizzas. To our boys, that was like a gourmet meal. They loved it.

Our dear friends, Glenn and Dee Simmons, came from Dallas bringing us their prayers, unconditional love and financial support. Glenn, a corporate executive, sat on the floor next to the bed and colored with Gabrielle for hours at a time. Dee was a constant source of encouragement and help to Cheryl with guidance relating to diet and nutrition to supplement the medical treatments.

Vicki Jamison-Peterson came day after day and simply laid her hands on Gabrielle's head and prayed quietly in the Spirit. Gabrielle just went about her activities coloring and playing with her Barbies. Still, she would ask, "Is that lady coming today?"

Lindsay and Richard Roberts were right by our sides whenever we needed them. They flew back and forth to Houston when we were at the clinic with Gabrielle. They were with us for every MRI. Lindsay supplied wonderful, organically grown vegetables from her garden and cooked many, many meals for us. They were with us every day bringing gifts, supplies and always their prayers. They graciously and lovingly became willing targets for Gabrielle's Super Soaker.

After Gabrielle's collapse in Michigan in July, it became more and more difficult to get her out of bed. Her equilibrium must have been out of kilter, and she was fearful even to get near the edge of the bed. Her world revolved around our bedroom and bathroom.

One night we went to Eastman Curtis's church without her. The people at church had made up big gift baskets for each of our children, including big Super Soaker water guns. Gabrielle was thrilled and giggled for all she was worth as she soaked every moving target that entered our bedroom and bathroom. Unfortunately, the wallpaper got more than its share of soaking as well. We said, "Gabrielle, we've got to get you outside with this Super Soaker."

"I'll go outside if I can squirt Aunt Lindsay and Uncle Richard."

We carried her down the steps and outside, where she waited with great anticipation. When Richard and Lindsay arrived and stepped out of their car, she unloaded on them and laughed and laughed. That became almost a daily event, and it solved our problem of trying to get her out in the fresh air.

The day Gabrielle went home to be with Jesus, Eastman and Angel were at the house. I boxed up her Super Soaker and said to them, "What you did for our daughter with this was priceless. I want you to have this." Those two people were sent to our family to take us out of captivity. We didn't even know them prior to Gabrielle's illness. At first I had thought, *This guy can't be real. Nobody can be so stinkin' happy all of the time.* The night Eastman showed up when Gabrielle's kidneys shut down, I said, "Eastman, wipe that grin off your face. It's not a good night." But you couldn't get that grin off his face, because he was there to bring joy.

Richard and Lindsay were the first to arrive the morning Gabrielle went home. Then came Billy Joe and Sharon Daugherty, Eastman and Angel Curtis, Kenneth and Lynette

Hagin and so many more. God knew who needed to be there. Lindsay was there for all of us. Billy Joe was there for Little Harry. They have a great relationship. Eastman was there for Roman. They are like two peas in a pod. Sharon helped clean up and set things right in a motherly manner. Richard was there to go to the funeral home with me, and then came the Hagins to comfort Cheryl.

A Final Good-Bye

I gathered everyone around our bed and said, "I remember we did this for my dad. I want everyone to say goodbye to Gabrielle. If you have to cry, I want you to get it out." Cheryl said good-bye to her; Nanny said good-bye; my mom, Stephanie, Lindsay, Roman, Harry, Richard and so forth—each one of us said goodbye. We all had our time to tell her we loved her and would see her soon.

So many people say, "We never got to say good-bye." I sincerely believe people need to do this. You don't have to be there at that physical moment of death to do it. A friend shared that she went back to her mother's grave and finally said good-bye after she got an understanding of this. She said, "When I did this, I finally got out of grief for my mom."

Seed Was in the Ground

The Friday before Gabrielle's home-going, some 50 to 100 people visited from all over America and Canada. One pastor and his wife from Canada flew in just to sit with our family for three days. God used all of these people, because we had seed in the ground with them. We had planted seed in their ministries and in their personal lives in a variety of ways. It is so important to get good seed in the ground, because when you have a need, God will bring those people across your path.

The body of Christ is jointly fit together for a purpose—to work together as one and to give to one another. If we want the body of Christ to be jointly fit to us, we have to *do* something to join ourselves to them. Otherwise, we are just a pile of bones, not accomplishing anything for the kingdom of God. We need joints and ligaments to tie us all together so we can do what God has called us to do. There is no such thing as a lone ranger in the kingdom of God. God intends for the body of Christ to operate as one body. No one should be alone. No one should be in want.

The body of Christ is jointly fit together for a purpose—to work together as one and to give to one another.

When we are faced with tests and trials, it is people of the kingdom of God who show up. Not one person from Cheryl's Miss America connections showed up at our house or did anything for us, except for Terry Meeuwesen, who is a former Miss America and is now co-host on the 700 Club. Terry called and prayed because she is a sister in the Lord, not because she was a Miss America sister. I had run a multi-million dollar organization, but not one business connection showed up. The world doesn't care. It was the people of God who were there for us at all hours of the day and night. The body of Christ must come to the aid of the body to give it life *and* to the aid of the world to save the world from dying.

The body of Christ must come to the aid of the body to give it life and to the aid of the world to save the world from dying.

We already shared with you how sixteen pastors and their wives came to the hospital in Michigan when Gabrielle collapsed. Two of these pastors, Dave and Mary Jo Williams, stayed with us nonstop during those days we were at the hospital. That first night was traumatic, and we were crowded into a tiny little waiting area near the intensive care unit. I was freezing cold, and Dave literally took the shirt off his back and made me put it on (coffee stains and all). That is a true brother. That is the family of God standing together as one.

Reach Out and Touch Someone

When someone is sick or in need, nothing that you do is too much or too little. Reach out and do whatever you are able to do. It may be prayer or an encouraging phone call. It may be cooking a meal or cleaning a house. It may be taking kids out to McDonalds or to a movie. It may be just being there to sit quietly by someone's side. Whatever the Lord impresses on you to do, do it!

Our friends Kay and Dan Newberry came to the house often. She would wash the dishes, do laundry or make beds. One day I came downstairs and Dan was running the vacuum. I said, "Why are you vacuuming?"

"Well, the lawn was already mowed so I thought I would do some vacuuming."

They just needed to come and do something, and they blessed us, as did many, many others.

The morning of Gabrielle's home-going our family was all with us, and I shared with you already how others came as well. After Gabrielle's body had been taken out of the house, I walked into our bedroom, and Sharon Daugherty was stripping the linens off the bed, vacuuming the room and getting rid of all of the medical supplies. She helped pick out an outfit for Gabrielle while we gathered special items from each family member to put in the casket, such as Cheryl's Bible, with this note on the inside cover: "When you get caught up in the air, wait for me"; a WWJD bracelet Roman picked out to match her outfit; a ring and angel necklace my mom had given to her; a blanket Cheryl's mom had made for her; and a doll from Little Harry and Roman that laughs when you jiggle it. (We knew if we heard that doll giggle during the celebration service that

Gabrielle was coming out of that casket healed and whole. God said it will happen in the last days, and we had the faith to believe for it!) It seemed our friends and family felt nothing was too much to do for us, and their thoughtful deeds of love restored our souls at a time when we were empty and spilled out.

It seemed our friends and family felt nothing was too much to do for us, and their thoughtful deeds of love restored our souls at a time when we were empty and spilled out.

Because of our public profile and previous security problems, we were advised not to leave Gabrielle's body alone or unattended. The funeral home made a special provision to allow one very special man, Louis Waller, to stay with our daughter all night in the funeral home. This was a great comfort to Roman, because Gabrielle had never been out of our sight. Louis stayed with her until her body was interned. Then he called me aside and said, "I'm going home now."

I am forever indebted to Louis for his sacrifice of love and dedication. Gabrielle loved Louis because this six-foot-plus tall, ex-Marine was her friend *and* because he baked her lemon bundt cake, which was her favorite. God provided for our special needs with special people for a special little girl.

Get Rid of Pride

One point I want to make is that we should never be too embarrassed or too proud to allow others to minister to us. Pride cuts off the opportunity both to bless and to be blessed. What if we had been too embarrassed to allow others to wash our dishes or do our laundry? We could not have kept up with everything alone, and we needed the love and care of others around us to keep us going. Restoration comes when we allow God to meet our needs—no matter how big or how small—through other people around us.

God never ceased to amaze us with how He could do this. We were ministering at a church in Zachary, Louisiana, with some very special friends, Rocky and Jodi Bezet, whose true pastor's hearts are a wonderful example of God's loving family. Gabrielle was due to have an MRI so that doctors could monitor what was happening with the tumor. Rocky and his family are some of our closest friends, and somehow they arranged through a church member to have a portable MRI unit brought to us so we didn't have to take Gabrielle to a strange hospital. When an eighteen-wheel tractor-trailer, with an MRI unit inside, pulled up in the parking lot decorated with balloons and "Wahoo!" posters, Gabrielle was thrilled. She loved parties for whatever reason, and the party atmosphere dispelled her dread of having the scan taken.

Another time when we went to minister with Rocky and Joni, we walked in our hotel rooms to find them decorated with balloons and "Wahoo!" posters. There were gift baskets for each of the children filled with toys and goodies. Gabrielle came in our room carrying her basket (she was still walking at that time) and said, "Daddy, this was in my basket." She handed me an envelope, turned and walked away. Inside the envelope was a $3000 check. It was so special how they did that. It wasn't about the money. It was that they had taken time to do something special for her and the boys.

Restoration comes by reaching out and helping someone else through prayer, little acts of kindness, serving a special need or giving toward a financial need. It takes your focus off your problems and onto doing what Jesus did. No matter how tired or stressed we were from taking care of Gabrielle, we were always restored when we ministered to others in the services we conducted.

God uses people to restore us, and He uses us to restore others. Job was restored when he prayed for his friends. (Job 42:10.) Do you need restoration? Are you willing to let Him use you to restore someone else? Take inventory of what God has given you and then step out and *do* something for someone else. As you restore others, God will restore you. Not only that, but you will find joy and fulfillment as you are jointly fit together with others doing what you were created and called to do in the kingdom of God.

A Glimpse of Heaven

by Vicki Jamison-Peterson

Angels who were watching at the portal descended to meet me, and I beheld in the near distance, a scene that can never fade from my memory.[1]

—REBECCA RUTER SPRINGER

It was Saturday evening, the end of a tiring day. There had been many boxes to pack and an unending stream of visitors—many saying, "I gave her that," quickly taking the object with them. My dear friend had gone to heaven, and I was deeply grieving. I had never been responsible for the details of a funeral, nor had I dealt with people who can be unusual on such occasions. My heart was crushed, but I needed rest.

A quotation from Longfellow is comforting when we think of precious Gabrielle:

She is not dead—the child of our affection—but gone
   unto that school

Where she no longer needs our poor protection, And
   Christ Himself doth rule.

Day after day, we think of what she is doing
    In those bright realms of air;

Year after year, her tender steps pursuing,
    Behold her grown more fair.[2]

After a long day of packing possessions, I saw a small gold book on her bookshelf and began to read of the glory of heaven described in this book, *Intra Muros*. Joy filled my heart. Thus, I began a long journey of "heaven breaks." I often reread *Intra Muros*, which tells of this woman's dream of heaven. Heaven must be built into our hearts, and it can be done.

Let me take you back to portions of *Intra Muros* for your own heaven break. Perhaps you need to be reminded that this life is short and there is a much greater one awaiting you who know and love the Lord.

> Someone was standing by me, and, when I looked up, I saw it was my husband's favorite brother, who "crossed the flood" many years ago.
>
> "My dear brother Frank!" I cried out joyously, "how good of you to come!"
>
> "It was a great joy to me that I could do so, little sister," he said gently. "Shall we go now?" and he drew me toward the window.... My brother drew me gently, and I yielded, passing with him through the window, out on the veranda, and from thence, in some unaccountable way, down to the street.... He had drawn my hand within his arm, and endeavored to interest me as we walked. But my heart clung to the dear ones whom I felt

I was not to see again on earth, and several times I stopped and looked wistfully back the way we had come. He was very patient and gentle with me, waiting always till I was ready to proceed again; but at last my hesitation became so great that he said pleasantly:

"You are so weak, I think I had better carry you;" and without waiting for a reply, he stooped and lifted me in his arms, as though I had been a small child; and, like a child, I yielded, resting my head upon his shoulder, and laying my arm about his neck. I felt so safe, so content, to be thus in his care. It seemed so sweet, after the long, lonely struggle, to have someone assume the responsibility of caring thus tenderly for me.[3]

Beneath the trees, in many happy groups, were little children, laughing and playing, running hither and thither in their joy, and catching in their tiny hands the bright-winged birds that flitted in and out among them, as though sharing in their sports, as they doubtless were…. As I looked upon their happy faces and their spotless robes, again I thought, "These are they who have washed their robes, and made them white in the blood of the Lamb."[4]

I was on the way to the river, my voice joined to the wonderful anthem of praise everywhere sounding, I saw a lovely young girl approaching me swiftly, with outstretched arms.

"Dear, dear Aunt Bertha!" she called, as she drew near, "do you not know me?"

"My little Mae!" I cried, gathering the dainty creature into my arms. "Where did you spring from so suddenly, dear? Let me look at you again!" holding her a moment at arm's length, only to draw her again tenderly to me.

"You have grown very beautiful, my child. I may say this to you here without fear, I am sure. You were always lovely; you are simply radiant now. Is it this divine life?"

"Yes," she said modestly and sweetly; "but most of all the being near the Savior so much."

"Ah, yes, that is it—being near Him! That will make any being radiant and beautiful," I said.

"He is so good to me; so generous, so tender!"

"He knows you love Him, dear heart; that means everything to Him."

"Love Him! Oh, if loving Him deserves reward, I am sure I ought to have every wish of my heart, for I love Him a thousandfold better than anything in earth or heaven."

The sweet face grew surpassingly radiant and beautiful as she talked, and I began to dimly understand the wonderful power of Christ among the redeemed in heaven. This dear child, so lovely in all mortal graces, so full of earth's keenest enjoyments during the whole of her brief life—pure and good, as we count goodness below, yet seemingly too absorbed in life's gaieties to think deeply of the things she yet in her heart revered and honored, now in this blessed life counted the privilege of loving Christ, of being near Him, beyond every other joy! And how that love refined and beautified the giver! As a great early love always shines through the face and elevates the whole character of the one who loves, so this divine love uplifts and glorifies the giver,

212

until not only the face but the entire person radiates the glory that fills the heart.[5]

Do you know, I think one of the sweetest proofs we have of the Father's loving care for us is that we so often find in this life the things which gave us great happiness below. The more unexpected this is, the greater joy it brings. I remember once seeing a beautiful little girl enter heaven, the very first to come of a large and affectionate family. I afterward learned that the sorrowful cry of her mother was, "Oh, if only we had someone there to meet her, to care for her!" She came, lovingly nestled in the Master's own arms, and a little later, as He sat, still caressing and talking to her, a remarkably fine Angora kitten, of which the child had been very fond, and which had sickened and died some weeks before, to her great sorrow, came running across the grass and sprang directly into her arms, where it lay contentedly. Such a glad cry as she recognized her little favorite, such a hugging and kissing as that kitten received, made joy even in heaven! Who but our loving Father would have thought of such comfort for a little child? She had evidently been a timid child; but now as the children gathered about her, with the delightful freedom they always manifest in the presence of the beloved Master, she, looking up confidently into the tender eyes above her, began to shyly tell of the marvelous intelligence of her dumb pet, until at last Jesus left her contentedly playing among the flowers with the little companions who had gathered about her. Our Father never forgets us, but provides pleasures and comforts us all, according to our individual needs.[6]

Take Your Place at the King's Table

by Harry Salem

A re you eating at the children's table or at the King's table? God has prepared a banquet table for us to dine at with Him, but too often we have not come up to a high enough level of spiritual maturity to enjoy its benefits. We are still assigned to the children's table, whining and complaining and perhaps even throwing food on the floor, because we don't like what is happening in our lives. I didn't realize that was where I was, until one day at church God spoke to me about my attitude.

God Uses a Bad Day

Shortly after Gabrielle's home-going, a ministry date in New York was cancelled because of bad weather, with temperatures at thirty degrees below zero and nine inches of snow. I believe God ordained that storm because He needed to have a talk with me. Whenever we are at home, we rotate our home churches between Rhema with Pastor Hagin, Victory Christian Center with Pastor Billy Joe and Sharon Daugherty, and Destiny with Pastor Eastman Curtis. This particular weekend we had already attended Destiny on Saturday night and planned to go to Victory Christian on Sunday morning and to Rhema that night. But that morning the Lord said, *No, you are to go to Rhema this morning.* When I walked into church that Sunday morning, I was mad! I couldn't even go to the church I wanted to that day. (I'm being honest. We all have our bad days.)

The ushers sat us in the front row. Brother Hagin began to speak. Let me paraphrase what he said:

> You know, God performs miracles. When our son was diagnosed with a brain tumor the size of your fist in the back of his head, the surgeons operated on him for twelve hours and got 80 percent of it out. We prayed and believed, and the rest of the tumor disappeared. We got our miracle!

Then he turned and saw us sitting there, and I believe he must have wished anybody had been sitting there that day but us. I was already mad, and what he had just said didn't make me any happier. He tried to go back to the podium to finish his message, but he couldn't go on. I saw him head in our direction, and I said, "Cheryl, he's coming after us."

The video cameras followed him as he came to us, and there we were on the big screens in front of the whole congregation. Everyone knew what we had been through, because they'd all prayed and stood with us. (This was the last place Gabrielle had sung.)

A Mark of Your Ministry

By this time Brother Hagin was standing right in front of us and saying, "I don't normally do this in church, but I've got to say this. If these people can sit in the front row, smiling, raising their hands and praising the Lord (I knew he was talking about Cheryl at that point) after what they have been through, then whatever you are going through, you can make it!" Then he turned and said, "And that will be a mark of your ministry. Don't quit and don't stop. You are doing something significant for God!"

I thought, *That's fine. It's a mark of our ministry.* But I was still mad.

We'd had lunch the day before with three ministers, and they had shared how God was blessing them. One had a new building; and another shared that he has four or five people who support him regularly with five, ten, and twenty thousand dollars a month. The other one had just gotten an airplane. As they talked, this is what had run through my mind: *He got my airplane. We're beating over the highway for thousands of miles, and we need an airplane as much as he does. Why don't we have a new building? Our ministry outgrew our*

*location a long time ago. And we sure could use some big
supporters like that. These guys haven't been through half of
what we've been through.* I was mad as could be at God, and,
believe me, no one wanted to be around me.

Have you ever looked at your neighbor and thought,
*He's got a brand new car and a new boat, and he's not even a
Christian. He's a heathen. And here I am driving a rattletrap!
Besides that, his kids are wearing $150 Nike shoes, and I'm
shopping at Payless. This stinks!*

Reaching Spiritual Maturity

There I was sitting in church still stewing over
yesterday's conversation and mad because I don't have an
airplane, big supporters or a new building. Even Brother
Hagin's message could not penetrate my bad attitude that
morning. That is when God started to talk to me. He had
only done that one other time in my life.

He said, *Harry.*

"Yeah."

*On November 23, when Gabrielle came home, you became
a man.*

"God, this isn't helping me. I've been a man since I was
nine years old when my father died."

No, on November 23 you became a spiritual man.

"What do you mean, God?"

You have gone to a new level with Me.

217

"I don't understand, God."

Let Me give you a visual so you will understand what I am saying. When you were a little boy at Thanksgiving, where did you eat dinner?

"I ate at the Thanksgiving table. Well, not really. I ate at the children's table, a card table, sitting on the piano bench with no cushion." I was thinking, *This isn't helping, God. I didn't like it back then. We all wanted to sit at the big table with the adults where the turkey was, eating off the fancy china plates and drinking from the crystal glasses that pinged when you tapped them.*

What did you eat? He asked.

"Mama fixed my plate and served me a child's portion."

On November 23 you graduated from the children's table, and even the adult's table, to the King's table.

"That's fine, God, but I still don't have an airplane or a nice building or that kind of supporters." He already knew what I was thinking, so I knew I might as well speak it aloud.

That's not My fault, Harry. I have you placed at the King's table, but you're still expecting child's portions. The problem is that you're in competition with those men, when you're supposed to be in covenant with them. You've got to make it right. Go back and apologize to them. When you start rejoicing with them, then I will bless you from the King's table and meet your specific needs, because you have been through something, son.

Competition Versus Covenant

Too many times we get into competition with other Christians and start coveting what they have. That is childish behavior, and God can't bless us when we act that way. I went back to all three of those men and apologized for my attitude and selfishness. It wasn't easy, but I did it so God could move on my behalf to meet my needs.

God has a pattern by which He does things on this earth, and His pattern never varies. We have to line up with His pattern in order for Him to bless us.

We can go through hell and back and be at a place where God is elevating us to a new level of inheritance and ruin it by what comes out of our mouths, by having a bad attitude or by focusing on someone else when we should be focusing on God. God has a pattern by which He does things on this earth, and His pattern never varies. We have to line up with His pattern in order for Him to bless us.

No More Child's Portions

Since that conversation with God, I am more conscientious about keeping my attitude right. However, one time I caught myself slipping back into that old mentality of expecting a child's portion.

219

My sister Lindsay set her faith on a new car. Her old car was eight years old, and it was a dog. I told her, "Don't you park that in my driveway again. I'm tired of wiping up your oil stains."

One day I received a phone call from a man who was coming up from Texas. He said, "You have to get Richard and Lindsay out to the car dealership at eight o'clock on Tuesday morning."

I knew we were to be at a board meeting on Tuesday morning at nine o'clock, so when I saw them at dinner that night I said, "Cheryl and I need you to come with us on Tuesday morning, but I'll have you back in time for the meeting."

They picked us up Tuesday morning, and we arrived at the dealership on time. A businessman Lindsay had never even met before handed Lindsay the keys to a brand new Lexus suv. Later at the board meeting, Lindsay shared her testimony about the new vehicle but didn't mention what kind it was. A man came up to her after the meeting and said, "I don't know what kind of vehicle it is, but I will pay your insurance for the next five years."

Cheryl and I rejoiced with Lindsay. She had waited upon the Lord and put her faith into action. We told her she needed to put a sign on it that said "Miracle!"

At the time this happened, Cheryl and I had given away our van a few months earlier as a seed for an airplane and hadn't replaced our vehicle yet. I caught myself thinking,

What is she going to do with her old car? The devil whispered in my ear and said, *Well, maybe she'll give you her old car.*

I recognized the deception and said, "No, I'm not accepting anything from the children's table ever again. God hasn't blessed us with another vehicle or our airplane yet, but when He does, each one will be from the King's table, I can tell you that!"

Take a Stand Against the Devil

When Gabrielle graduated to heaven and then Cheryl was diagnosed with cancer, I took my stand against the devil and said, "We're not taking anymore. I'm drawing a line in the sand. I'm not letting this happen anymore." I was not going to back up or accept anything less than a King's portion.

When Little Harry was still small enough for us to call him that, I said, "Son, when you make a stand for something, you draw a line in the sand and don't back up."

One day Cheryl called me and said, "Meet me at the doctor's office." By the tone of her voice, I knew something was wrong.

"What's wrong?"

"Meet me at the doctor's office, and I'll tell you then."

I walked into the doctor's office, and there sat Little Harry with an ice pack on his head. I looked at Cheryl and said, "What's the matter?"

"Ask *your* son!" I could tell by the way she'd said, *"your* son," that I was in hot water.

"Little Harry, what happened to your head?"

"I need stitches, Daddy."

"Why?"

When you draw a line in the sand and take a stand, Satan has a rock waiting for you, but God is bigger than that rock.

"Well, you know how you told me to draw a line in the sand and never step back?"

"Yeah."

"Well, a kid came and drew a line in the sand and said, 'Step over that line, and I'll hit you in the head with a rock.'"

"What happened?"

"I stepped over the line, but you said never to step back so I didn't, and he hit me in the head with a rock!"

When you draw a line in the sand and take a stand, Satan has a rock waiting for you, but God is bigger than that rock. Are you ready to take a stand to keep your attitude right and move to your rightful place at the King's table?

Mature to the Level of Your Inheritance

Your Father God has left an inheritance for you, but you won't receive it until you mature to the level of your inheritance. It is being held in trust for you until that time. In the world, the assets of a legal trust are held and not released until the beneficiary of the trust reaches a certain age of maturity. It works the same way with God. If you want to stay at the children's table sitting on the piano bench, that's your choice; but there is an appointed time for you to be elevated to the level of your inheritance, to take your place at the King's table. That time is *now!* Trust Him and see if He doesn't pour out a blessing so great that you won't be able to contain it!

Your Father God has left an inheritance for you, but you won't receive it until you mature to the level of your inheritance.

A Crown of Jewels

by Stephanie (Salem) Cantees

Dear Gabs:

Your mom and I kept "diaries." So many things happened that without them, I was afraid we might forget something. This seems like the appropriate time to say what stood out more vividly than anything else I remember.

It happened the night in Kalamazoo, Michigan, when we were at the hospital to which you had been flown on the Life Flight helicopter. Your daddy was standing outside by the motor coach, and he wanted so much for Aunty Lindy to come. I walked with him, and we talked. I could feel the intensity of how much he relied on Aunt Lindy's spiritual strength.

As we walked, the halos from the lights in the hospital parking lot seemed to illuminate, casting almost a radiant beam. It was around 1:00 A.M. and we were weary, but I knew the two figures coming forward contained the life raft your daddy so wanted. Dave (Pastor Tipover) and Mary Jo Williams came right to your daddy. Your daddy literally fell into "Pastor Tipover's" arms and wept. As I stood back and watched, I knew that your daddy's mantle from heaven was fully descending upon him. (See 2 Kings 2:1-15.) From that moment on, I knew your daddy was moved into the position of his spiritual calling. He came into his own. I cannot put into words what my spirit sensed, but as I saw the transformation emerge, it was incredible. I saw him go from a participant uncertain of his merit to the spiritual leader he was called to be. His respect for Aunt Lindy's spiritual strength never diminished, but I watched him reach within to re-embrace his own spiritual strength.

I often wonder if the mechanical problems of the airplane that kept Aunt Lindy from getting to Kalamazoo weren't ordained for a reason. Without Lindy being there, I think it allowed your daddy's transformation. Pastor Tipover, Mary Jo, Gary, Patti, Ron Clark—we all saw your daddy's spiritual leadership burst forth. I, as others, am convinced this was the spiritual turning point of leadership for your daddy.

Gabrielle, that Miss America crown your mommy won, and you so loved to look at to see all the "sparkle" and "diamonds," must seem pretty small compared to the one you have. Do you wonder how come it seems to get bigger and bigger with more jewels? You see, every time your daddy, mommy or brothers lead another person to the Lord, another jewel "grows in your crown." Sweet baby, you, my precious goddaughter, had such a purpose, and it is going on and on and on.

Jesus said, "I have gone ahead to prepare a place."
(John 14:2.) Oh, Gabs, how I remember the many times I'd
come every night to sleep at your house in what was to be
"auntie's" bed in the blue room and the little gifts you
plotted and placed in my bed. I will never forget the look
on your face as you'd grin when I asked if there was
anything in my bed. At only six, you had little Roman
planting bugs, spiders and frogs there. In the midst of it all,
Gabs, you were still a feisty little doll. I can only imagine
the "planning and plotting" you are doing as you have
gone ahead to prepare me a place there in heaven.

With all my love,
Auntie

Dad-to-Dad

by Harry Salem

It was "love at first sight" when I looked into the deep blue eyes of the most beautiful girl in the world during the early morning hours of May 26, 1993. Gabrielle Christian Salem captured her daddy's heart forever. I was surprised at the depth of my emotions for this little pink bundle of joy.

My dad died when I was only nine years old, and so I grew up surrounded by girls—my mom and two sisters. I always thought I wanted a family of boys. When Cheryl's ultrasound revealed we were to have a daughter, it took me a little while to adjust my thinking. However, when I held *my daughter* in my arms for the first time, I could have sung that old song, "Thank heaven for little girls!"—if I could sing, that is. I am so blessed that God allowed me to experience such a love.

She Knew Her Purpose

Gabrielle came into this world with an "attitude," and it didn't take long for her to let everyone in the family know what her role was going to be. Her giggles and quick wit kept us laughing, even when she was doing something she wasn't supposed to do. Her persistence and determination showed us how to press in and never give up, no matter how difficult the task might be. She kept us all in line and made sure everyone was dressed just *right*, with hair combed and ready on time for whatever activity or event was on the schedule. She turned everything into a party and never wanted anyone to be left out of the fun. She was a giver of life to everyone with whom she came in contact. Most of all, she knew her purpose in God's kingdom and never passed up a chance to tell others about her Jesus.

Gabrielle came into this world with an "attitude," and it didn't take long for her to let everyone in the family know what her role was going to be.

My Hero, Gabrielle

Gabrielle was truly my hero as I watched her courageously walk through the final year of her life with

such grace and mercy. It truly did break my heart to hand
her over to Jesus after only six years. In my humanness as a
daddy, I wanted to see her grow up and, yes, even walk
down the aisle to be married to the man of God's choosing.
The time that we had with her seemed so short, and yet I
have peace in my heart knowing she is in a place of
abounding love and joy unthinkable where there is no pain
and no tears.

Nothing Missing, Nothing Broken

The name *Salem* means "peace," and in Hebrew the word
peace means "nothing missing and nothing broken." A few
months ago I had a heavenly vision of Gabrielle resting on a
beautiful sofa bed. In heaven a day is as 1000 years on earth.
(2 Peter 3:8.) She didn't even know we were not there with
her. She was alive. Her eyes were open, and she could move
around; but she wasn't breathing as we do here on earth.
Thus, I knew she was in heaven. She was just resting and
being restored from all that she had been through. I believe
the Lord showed me that vision so I would be at peace and
be comforted. We are being restored just as she is. My heart
is no longer broken. I miss her, but nothing is broken and
nothing is missing because I know right where she is.

The Pain of Fatherhood

I am writing this chapter for fathers who are walking
through the tests and trials of life. I understand how hard it

seems at times to be strong for those around you when your own heart is breaking inside. I feel your pain. I stood at the bedside of my precious little darling and knew it was up to me to release her and hand her over to Jesus. Cheryl said to me afterward, "I wouldn't have let her take her last breath." I believe God made Cheryl go to sleep because I had to make the final decision.

The thought crossed my mind that Cheryl might resent me or be mad at me. The enemy so often uses blame to bring division. Someone has to be blamed, and often it is the one closest to you who becomes the target. It was a risk I had to take. I had to trust Cheryl to accept my decision.

I believe that no mother should have to watch her child die. I don't care how strong she is. A woman is a mender, and a man is a fixer. A woman always believes she can mend her child. The moment of death burns in your mind. As beautiful as it was to see Gabrielle blowing kisses and to see her facial features relax and return to normal, I still hear the hiss of the oxygen machine. I hear it every night. I fought putting her on oxygen because I knew someday I would have to turn it off, and I did.

When I woke Cheryl up and told her Gabrielle was gone, I stood by and watched her call out to Gabrielle's spirit to come back into her body for thirty minutes or more. I watched my nine-year-old son, Roman, lie on his sister's chest, put his hands on her cheeks and speak life into her for over fifteen minutes. I gathered my family around and prayed with them before calling the coroner to come. My heart was breaking, but I knew I had done what I had to do.

In Loving Hands

God was in charge of every step in this process. Dr. Mike Ritze, our family doctor, delivered our sweet Gabrielle into this world. As it turned out he was the coroner for Broken Arrow, and so he was the one to see her go out of this world as well. We are so grateful for Dr. Mike's loving support. He loved her and cried with us. Gabrielle was never in anybody else's hands other than those who knew and loved her. When I received the initial report from the ophthalmologist that there was pressure on her brain, I went across the hall to Dr. Mike's office and asked him to explain what was happening. The word that was rising up in my spirit was "tumor." Dr. Mike was not able to give me any definitive answers without further tests, but he was honest and forthright with me whenever I went to him for answers or advice.

In the weeks before Gabrielle's home-going, Dr. Mike helped me to understand in black and white what was taking place in Gabrielle's physical body. It prepared me for what was happening in the natural realm, and I was grateful for his help.

God's Sovereign Plan

We never stopped believing in God's supernatural healing power, but God had a sovereign plan. I received that truth when Oral Roberts came to our home four days before Gabrielle's home-going and spoke this prophetic word over our family:

Harry, here is what the Holy Spirit is saying to me in this critical hour:

You and Cheryl are in the fiery furnace. I have often wondered what the men looked like in that fiery furnace of Daniel's day. Now I am looking at two people in the midst of the fire. God did not put you there. Satan has been seeking to destroy your lives and your ministry.

We never stopped believing in God's supernatural healing power, but God had a sovereign plan.

But the fourth Man in that furnace has spoken to the fire and said, "You shall not burn their bodies or scorch their clothes or singe their hair. I am robbing the fire of its violence and subduing the fiery flames. I am breaking the power of a 'hit' on your life and ministry. Soon you will hear a voice saying, 'Come forth from the fire,' and never again will the enemy have the power to throw you into the fiery furnace."

Jesus said, "Suffer the little children to *come unto me* and forbid them not, for of such is the kingdom of God." [Mark 10:14] This has two meanings. First, let them come into My arms while I am here on earth, and second, let them come into my arms when I have returned to heaven. Little Gabrielle has been My specially anointed one. My love has shone through her, and I have healed many through her joyous heart and strong faith. I have glorified My name through her.

Now her suffering must come to an end. *Let her come unto Me!* Her presence with Me will be a bridge between you and heaven while you and the boys remain on earth to complete your ministry as powerful instruments of My love and compassion. There is no glory in watching her little body suffer more. It is time to let her go, to come unto Me.

Harry, I love you and Cheryl and Little Harry and Roman. I live in you. I affirm you, and you carry My anointing. Your vision will from the hour of Gabrielle's homecoming be equally of the ones in heaven and those on earth.

I must tell you, Gabrielle will be released very shortly. The hour is here. You must accept what you already know in your heart. When she is gone your grieving will soon be over, and Jesus will fill the aching void in your heart. You are Mine and I am yours, and nothing will ever come between us!

In response to this prophetic word, I said, "Oral, I receive this." I had to trust God with my daughter even to the point of releasing her and letting her go to Him. It was a heart-wrenching choice but, as the spiritual head of our home, I had to make it. Yes, I had faith to believe for her healing and even that she could be raised from the dead, but I had to trust God that His plan was best for Gabrielle. I had to trust God that we would come out of this fiery furnace with not so much as the smell of smoke on our clothing. I had to trust God that our grief would not linger, that Jesus would fill the terrible void in our hearts and that the Son would shine in the morning. Bottom line, I had to trust God!

Healing Tears

Men, I want you to know that it is okay to cry and it is okay to show your emotions. Tears heal. On his deathbed, my father charged me with being the man of the family when I was only ten years old. He told me men don't cry because it is a sign of weakness and never to show emotion in public. I lived up to his charge for many years. I was proud and stoic and never allowed my emotions to show on my countenance.

In my book *For Men Only* I share how God did a heart transplant on me and transformed me from being just a provider in my home to being a participant. The Harry Salem who is writing this book is not the same Harry Salem who ran the Oral and Richard Roberts' ministries and was vice-president of Oral Roberts University eight years ago. I am no longer afraid to let my emotions spill out. Even Jesus wept (John 11:35), so who are we as men to say that tears are a sign of weakness? Walking through the pain of the past two years has softened my heart even more and given me a greater capacity for compassion and love toward others who are suffering.

Even Jesus wept, so who are we as men to say that tears are a sign of weakness?

A Walk Through the Fire

Over the past eight years we have walked through many tests and trials. We lost our third son, Malachi Charles, in a miscarriage. Cheryl almost miscarried Gabrielle and then was confined to bed for seven months. Gabrielle was diagnosed with sleep apnea, which put her life in danger. Cheryl slipped into a deep depression brought on by a chemical imbalance in her body and almost died. Then came that fateful day—January 11, 1999—when our world turned upside down. The year that followed was truly a walk through the fire. Three months after Gabrielle's home-going, Cheryl went into surgery for colon cancer.

Through it all, God has been faithful to show me how to stand firm on His Word and how to develop an intimacy with Him so I could hear His voice and be led by His Spirit.

Are You a Spiritual Leader at Home?

If you haven't taken your rightful place as the spiritual head of your home, *now* is the time to step up to the plate and be the man God has called you to be. You can't do this unless you have Jesus living in your heart *and* have an intimate relationship with the Father. When you submit to God's authority, your wife and children will follow your lead, and order and peace will be restored in your home.

Too many men are sitting on the sidelines and letting their wives take care of the spiritual aspects of their homes. I know I did that for the first few years of our marriage.

Cheryl was strong in her knowledge of the Word and in spiritual gifts, and it was easy to just let her do it. It wasn't until depression tried to take her out that the rubber hit the road, and I realized I had to step out of my comfort zone and become the spiritual leader God meant for me to be. I had to read my Bible and pray so *I* could get closer to Him. I had to pull down the wall of protection I had built up around my heart, and just sit down and begin to talk to God about what I was feeling. Once I experienced this closeness with Him, I never wanted to go back to where I had been.

Two-way Communication

Once you begin to talk with God intimately and really communicate with Him, He will begin to talk to you and reveal things to you. As you read your Bible and start understanding Christian principles, you will soon learn how to hear His voice through the Scriptures and through prayer. Communication is a two-way street. When you talk, He listens; and when you are still and listen, He will talk to your spirit. When you give of yourself and your time, He gives back to you the desires of your heart.

God gives us the most powerful revelations when we commit to spend time with Him. Men who are casually interested in God do not receive the same revelations that committed men of faith receive, as it says in this Scripture:

> *But without faith it is impossible to please and be satisfactory*
> *to Him. For whoever would come near to God must [necessarily]*

believe that God exists and that he is the rewarder of those
who earnestly and diligently seek Him [out].

HEBREWS 11:6 AMP

I challenge you to make a commitment to earnestly and
diligently seek God with your whole heart. Make it a
heartfelt relationship that
will not let anything stop it
or stand in its way. You are a
King's kid, and He wants to
spend time with you. He
wants to bless you.

As you grow in your
knowledge and intimacy
with the Lord, you will be
prepared to stand in the gap
for your family and loved
ones. Remember what we
said earlier: You have to get

Men who are casually
interested in God do not
receive the same revelations
that committed men
of faith receive.

the Word into your heart *before* the crisis so that when you
are squeezed, it will come out. Don't delay taking action to
fill up on God's Word. The enemy strikes when you least
expect it. Don't put your family or yourself at risk by not
being prepared when the test comes.

Examine What You Do With Your Time

One more important word I have for dads is this: It is
not how long we have with our children on this earth that
counts; it is what we *do* with the time. I had to take over
the responsibilities of the children and the household

when Cheryl had to stay in bed during Gabrielle's pregnancy and then when she became so sick with depression in 1994. I soon discovered that I really didn't know my children at all. What a joy it was to spend time with each one as I gave them baths and tucked them into their beds at night. I learned how unique and wonderful they were as individuals. I had been missing the best years of their lives while I was working *"for the Lord."* God changed my priorities and my focus. Now I work *with* the Lord.

It is not how long we have with our children on this earth that counts; it is what we do with the time.

Life Is a Series of Moments

I wouldn't trade the time I have with Cheryl and our children for anything in the world. They are my heritage. They are the only things I can take to heaven with me. We only had six years with Gabrielle, but we literally spent every moment with her. I cherish those moments now that she is gone; but more than that, I am comforted by the fact that we will see her again and be with her for eternity.

Time Equals Love

How much time are you spending with your children individually and together? Fathers set the tone for the home.

If you don't spend time with your children, they won't spend time with you. Are you working day and night to provide for the physical needs of your family and sacrificing your time with those who need you most? We are often so busy doing things *for* our children that we forget to do anything *with* our children. Time equates to love in the

Time equates to love in the mind of a child.

mind of a child. Don't miss the opportunities to demonstrate your love to your family. They are your heritage and your treasure.

If you want to learn more about how to be a participant and not just a provider and how to step into your role as spiritual leader of your home, let me encourage you to read my book *For Men Only*.

Most importantly, find the courage to get close to your Father God. Pull your chair up close to Him. He is right there in the room with you. He loves you and wants to show you how to love and care for your family. Let Him teach you how to have a strong, happy family.

Testimony of a Christian Family

by Dr. J. Michael Ritze

I first met Harry and Cheryl years ago when they individually came to ORU to work for the ministry. I commented to my wife how blessed we were to have such talent and dedication at ORU. A short time after that, we learned they were to be husband and wife.

A few years later I became their family physician when they asked me to provide prenatal care and delivery of their son Roman. I received many blessings from this wonderful experience of witnessing firsthand the joy of a Christian family in the making. Cheryl was a wonderful wife and mother, and Harry was a fantastic husband and father. A few years later I had the joy of delivering Gabrielle into the world.

It was inspiring to watch the children growing up and maturing in the Lord as well. Salem Family Ministries was reaching out and touching so many for His glory. Their lives seemed to be like a storybook, until January 11, 1999, when I examined Gabrielle with some eye problems. My heart broke when I had to tell them the news of this malignant, inoperable brain tumor. I prayed with them and for them. This disease tested everyone's faith. In the proceeding months, I asked the Lord to give me strength as I saw Gabrielle being called to her heavenly home. Two days before Thanksgiving, she was promoted to heaven.

Harry and Cheryl honored me by asking me to be one of the pallbearers for Gabrielle's home-going celebration. I praise God for being allowed to know and love this family, especially Gabrielle Christian.

From a Mother's Heart

by Cheryl Salem

Every mother treasures certain special moments in life. On New Year's Day 1999 we took the children to see the movie *The Prince of Egypt*. As we were driving back to Tulsa after ministering in Mississippi and Alabama over the holidays, I looked over at Harry and said, "This is exactly what I have always wanted to do with my life. I've had our babies, and now we are ministering together and are happy." That moment in time was like a snapshot of a mother's heart full of love and contentment.

Needless to say, eleven days later when the doctors gave us the evil report about Gabrielle I was like a mother bear protecting her young. I had fought too hard to bring our baby girl into this world, and no devil was going to steal her from us. I had all of God's weapons and His angels on my side. I went into "attack mode" against a defeated foe. This wasn't the first time I had waged such a war, so I knew how to go about it. I engaged my faith and never wavered.

I had fought too hard to bring our baby girl into this world, and no devil was going to steal her from us. I had all of God's weapons and His angels on my side.

Imparting His Word

Being a mommy is the most fulfilling role a woman can play in life. I was even led to write a book titled *The Mommy Book* to help mothers put faith into action, pray with power over their children and to be encouraged in their pursuit of godly motherhood. One of the chapters speaks of the power of impartation, as the apostle Paul spoke of in this Scripture:

> For I am yearning to see you, that I may impart and share with you some spiritual gift to strengthen and establish you.

ROMANS 1:11 AMP

Webster's Dictionary defines the word *impart* as "to give a share of, to make known, communicate." When we realize that our children's spirits are able to receive so much at such an early age (even in the womb), we will understand the impact of the unlimited privilege we have to impart the Word of God to them.

When we realize that our children's spirits are able to receive so much at such an early age (even in the womb), we will understand the impact of the unlimited privilege we have to impart the Word of God to them.

As we impart the Word of God into our children by His Spirit, they comprehend great spiritual truths at an early age. I believe that all the time I spent in bed speaking the Word and praying over Gabrielle and having such quiet intimate times with the Lord while she was still in the womb, imparted to her a greater level of anointing than I have experienced in my own life.

Children Do What They See

It is important to remember that we do not impart *what we know*; we impart *who we are*. All of our children were taught of the Lord from the moment they were born; and as they watched Harry and I walk out our faith in the natural in everyday life, they received spiritual impartation from us to know how to receive the power of the Holy Spirit and how to speak the Word and pray with power over every need and circumstance. Gabrielle watched Harry and I, as well as her brothers, and received an impartation of power from all of us. She truly had a spiritual maturity far beyond her years.

Hold You Me!

Sometimes as mothers we feel as if we give and give and give. However, giving is not a one-way street. When we open our eyes and receive what our children have to give, they bless us beyond all measure. When Roman was about two years old, he would run up to me and grab me around my knees saying, "Hold you me." He wanted to hold me as much as he wanted me to hold him. When I was

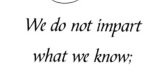

We do not impart

what we know;

we impart who we are.

battling depression back in 1994, Roman would slip out of bed at night and quietly tiptoe into our room. I would feel his little hand touch my cheek ever so softly as he whispered, "Mommy, I love you." There is nothing like the love of a little child. Children love us as the Father God does—unconditionally!

The Father God pours His love into our hearts through our children and ministers to us in great ways. He has used Young Harry to give me strength, Roman to give me joy and even used Malachi Charles (our baby who was miscarried) to give me a greater compassion. Gabrielle brought healing and restoration.

A Shadow at My Side

Once I overcame the fear of bringing a girl into this world, as I shared with you earlier, I discovered how much fun it was to have a little girl. She was my shadow and never left my side. We did all the "girl" things together—playing Barbies, putting on makeup and dressing up. She watched and imitated my every move. Harry says she was a mirror image of me. She had my eyes, my looks and my personality. For her the world was meant to be a party, and yet, there was always a tremendous depth to her spirituality. She was uniquely destined for greatness in the kingdom of God.

Children love us as the Father God does—unconditionally!

Pictures of Heaven

In July, right after Gabrielle collapsed in Michigan, I was talking with Kellie Copeland Kutz. Kellie asked me how much we talked with Gabrielle about heaven. I explained that we often taught the children about heaven and read books to them about how wonderful and beautiful it is. They loved Jesse Duplantis's book *Heaven: Close Encounters of the God Kind,* and I sometimes read to them excerpts of Rebecca Ruter Springer's book *Intra Muros,* "*My Dream of Heaven,*" such as this one:

> I think I must have slept; for the next I knew, I was sitting in a sheltered nook, made by flowering shrubs, upon the softest and most beautiful turn of grass, thickly

studded with fragrant flowers, many of them flowers I
had known and loved on earth. I remember noticing the
heliotrope, violets, lilies of the valley, and mignonette,
with many others of like nature wholly unfamiliar to me.
But even in that first moment I observed how perfect in
its way was every plant and flower.[1]

Kellie said, "Don't show Gabrielle any movies or read
any books to her about heaven or talk to her about people
in heaven. You've got to make her want to stay here on
earth. Children are supernatural minded and love Jesus
even more than we do. They want to be there in heaven
with Him. You need to prepare as a family or individually
to make a covenant with Gabrielle that she will stay here
on earth."

Sealed with a Covenant

I talked with Gabrielle about it, and we made a
covenant with each other, wrote it down and signed it that
she would not leave me and I would not leave her on this
earth. Then we took communion on it.

I knew from that point on, no matter how bad it got,
she wouldn't leave me. I had such great faith, and I knew
she was just like me—stubborn and strong. Gabrielle had a
tremendous, unearthly kind of faith. It was like my faith
developed at forty-three years old in her at six. She had an
understanding about spiritual matters. I didn't have to
explain it; she just got it!

Harry and the boys made their own covenants with her, and as a family we took communion at least once a week. The boys took turns preparing and leading communion (getting the crackers and juice, reading a Scripture and talking about it each time).

As I look back, I know the only reason she stayed with us from July through November was because of her promise and her faith. When Oral Roberts came to our home four days before her home-going and gave his word of prophecy that it was time to release her, Harry received it, but I couldn't do it. I was so angry at Oral that I left the room. I am being really honest. My mother's heart was not ready to let her baby go. I still believed God was going to give us a supernatural miracle and raise her up.

Free To Choose

Finally on Sunday, her body was shutting down, and we sensed in our spirits that she was slipping away from us. Harry and I talked, and as hard as it was, we finally agreed it was time to release her from our covenant. We knew that whether she stayed or went to heaven needed to be her choice, not ours.

I took her hand in mine and said, "Gabrielle, I know you and I made a promise to each other, but if you don't want to stay here, I understand. You can go or you can stay. If you want to go just praise the Lord, Mommy will be okay." She squeezed my hand, and I said, "I'll walk you as far as I can."

And the Angels Came

It may sound incredible, but I still didn't really think she would go. That last night I sat with her and saw the angels come three times, but I wasn't ready even then. That is why God had to put me to sleep. When Harry woke me up and said, "She's gone," I couldn't believe she had left me that quickly. For six years my world had been consumed with her. She was with me twenty-four hours a day, always my girl, my best friend. She loved life so much.

I realize I will not understand the "why?" until I see Him face-to-face, but I love Him and trust Him and that is enough for now.

One of the hardest things I struggled with after Gabrielle was gone was that I didn't know how to stop believing for her healing. I still stand for it in Jesus' name, because I know He did it. He just didn't do it *my* way. I realize I will not understand the "why?" until I see Him face-to-face, but I love Him and trust Him and that is enough for now.

Focus on What You Do Have

I am learning to deal with the pain of separation by coming up to a higher level in the spirit—being more heavenly minded—and I am learning how to get through each day without Gabrielle by focusing on what I *do* have rather than what I don't have. When I find myself having a bad day and feeling sorry for myself, I remind myself Gabrielle would be very disappointed and be the first one to correct me if she saw me acting that way. I spent six years training her to be happy all the time, which she was.

An Overcoming Victory

One of the biggest victories came for me one day while ministering in California. A mother came forward for prayer with her little girl, who was six or seven years old. This little girl had multiple brain tumors, though they weren't in the brainstem, and she was being given steroids. She had just begun to swell up from fluid retention, as Gabrielle had. It was a test of my faith to be able to pray for this little girl; but as I began to pray, the anointing came upon me. Harry and the boys laid hands on her and I began to sing over her.

It was such a relief to have that experience behind me. I didn't know how I would ever be able to pray for a little child with a brain tumor, but God was there in the midst of it all. Once I prayed for one child, I knew I could pray for others. It's like the first time you go back to the grave. The first time is a killer, but once it is over, you know you can do it again. I have this little girl in my prayer book, and I pray for her every day. I believe God that she is completely healed and restored.

One Day at a Time

We have to defeat each lie from the enemy and each painful memory one at a time. My faith is stronger than ever because I trust in the One who heals *all* of our infirmities. (Ps. 103:3.) Every time I stand and pray for others I know my prayer warrior, Gabrielle, is with me in spirit standing before the throne of God, where her presence is a bridge between heaven and me. Her destiny *is* being fulfilled as the Lord's name is glorified through her. That is why this mother will never stop testifying of His goodness and mercy. He is mine and I am His, and nothing will ever come between us!

Every time I stand and pray for others, I know my prayer warrior, Gabrielle, is with me in spirit standing before the throne of God, where her presence is a bridge between heaven and me.

I pray that whatever tests or trials you are facing, God will minister His peace to you. Reach out and find your rest in Him. Treasure those special moments you have with each family member and keep those snapshots in your heart. Focus on what you do have, not what you don't have, and speak the Word of God over your family and circumstances. Stand on His promises, because His Word does not return void. (Isa. 55:11.) Do what you can do today, and let Jesus take care of tomorrow. Most of all, trust Him because He cares for you.

Here is a special song Gabrielle and I sang together often. I hope it blesses the heart of every mother who reads it as much as it has blessed mine.

Bless You

Bless you, bless you, bless you, my mama.
Bless you, bless you, and bless you in His name.

Give you happiness, and laughter, and joy in your
heart, peace of mind, contentment. From His love
never part...

Bless you, bless you, bless you, my mama.
Bless you, bless you, and bless you in His name.

May God protect you and keep you, safe from all harm,
Give you a heart of love, strong in faith
When you've grown from my arms...

Bless you, bless you, bless you, my mama.
Bless you, bless you, and bless you in His name.

Keep you honest and sure, faithful and true of the
blessing I pray for your life.

Bless you, bless you, bless you, my mama.
Bless you, bless you, and bless you in His name.

Bless you, bless you, bless you, my baby.
Bless you, bless you, and bless you in His name.

"Gabrielle Christian Salem, may the Lord bless you and
keep you.

May He make His face to shine upon you and give you
peace.

Gabrielle, may He bring you happiness, love, joy and
health.

Gabrielle Christian Salem, I bless you!"

"I Bless You, Mommy!"[2]

A Gift of Remembrance

by Dee and Glenn Simmons

It hurts to lose someone you love, someone who has a special place in your heart. It hurts when you awake in the morning; it hurts in the middle of the day, in the dark of the night and once again when morning brings reality. Gabrielle Christian Salem was a special person in our lives.

In the eleven months Gabrielle was ill, we had several opportunities to spend time with her to make memories. During these special visits we played Barbies. After all, Gabrielle was "the Barbie queen." Glenn cherishes the day he sat by her bed on the floor and the two of them colored together. Her courage, her strength, her joy and, most of all, her faith brought to our lives the meaning of life. She knew when to let go and when to say good-bye. Gabrielle taught us to honor and to accept the gift of remembrance as she completed her journey and made a successful closing.

Several years ago I lost my best friend—my mother—to cancer. I learned grieving is a natural part of closing. However, I often wonder where the tears of grief end and the tears of joy begin.

I will never forget the day Gabrielle and I said our good-byes. The date was Thursday, November 18, 1999. The time was 3:00 P.M. I was attending an ORU board meeting. Suddenly, urgency engulfed me. *I must go and see her today!* I went to my friend, Lindsay Roberts, told her I must leave and asked her to please take me to Gabrielle.

As I entered Harry and Cheryl's bedroom, where Gabrielle lay propped up on pillows, I knelt by her side. The next two hours I spent talking to, hugging and praying for her from my heart. Gabrielle taught us all about love. Her voice was weak, but the love radiating from her eyes was so powerful that they said, "I love you!" She was able to comfort me as we said good-bye. I knew the heavenly hosts were hovering all around. I could actually feel the swish of angels' wings, and I knew this would be the last visit I would share with her on this earth—the next time I would hold her she would have a healed, glorified little body. At that moment I began to sing "Something Beautiful, Something Good"—the same song I sang as my mother entered the heavenly gates. The end of the song says, "He made something beautiful of my life." Surely He made something beautiful of Gabrielle's life.

November 19, 1999, at 10:00 A.M. Glenn went to see Gabrielle for his final visit. He shared with me that he was happy God gave him one more visit. Closing is not always saying good-bye. Closing also means saying good night.

The call came early Tuesday morning, November 23. The angels had descended, and Gabrielle Christian Salem was now singing a solo in the heavenly choir. Through the eleven months of illness, Gabrielle never let the devil steal her song. It is easy to sing when you are on a mountaintop, when your life is happy and carefree and everything is coming up roses; but she kept singing no matter how bad she felt. Over 100 times during that eleven-month battle, she carried her backpack right up on the platform and sang her heart out. When she couldn't get out of bed any longer, she kept singing and playing her little keyboard. She was a unique and specially anointed child who knew her purpose and her mission in life. She changed the world and the people around her. She changed me.

In January 1999 I was walking in a dark valley. I had to make a decision whether to sell my nutrition company, Ultimate Living. An excellent offer had been made and my precious husband, Glenn, felt we should accept it. I was torn over what to do. I knew God had given me a ministry to help others live healthy, prosperous lives, but I was weary. Glenn really wanted me to retire and travel around the world with him. I just kept praying and asking the Lord for direction.

When Harry and Cheryl took Gabrielle to the clinic in Houston the first time, Glenn and I met them there. We loved them so much, and we just wanted to be with them. While I went with Harry and Cheryl into the doctor's office, Glenn stayed in the reception area with our dear friend, Lindsay Roberts. He shared with Lindsay that we were considering selling Ultimate Living. Lindsay was shocked and said, "What? Ultimate Living isn't just a platform; it's her ministry. She can't sell her anointing! Mama and I are going to pray about this."

A few days later Lindsay called and said, "We have prayed, and you are *not* to sell Ultimate Living. It is your anointing and your ministry!" She confirmed in my heart what the Lord had been trying to tell me. I had peace at last.

I went to Glenn and said, "Honey, I'm not going to sell Ultimate Living."

He looked at me and said, "Not at any price?"

"Not at any price!"

Through Gabrielle Christian Salem's life God took my vision, my mission and my passion to a new commitment, a new dimension and a new level.

Many times I close my eyes and see Gabrielle. When I listen to the wind I hear her. Because we truly loved her, she will always be here. It's the gift of remembrance that the Master of all gives to those of us left behind.

In my heart I know my mother is Gabrielle's heavenly grandmother. How do I know? I warned her Gabrielle was on the way. With Gabrielle's spirit and zest for life, mother needed to be on alert. Gabrielle has a special radar, and there is no doubt that she is directing the parade all over heaven.

Yes, Gabrielle's life lives on as we choose to celebrate her beautiful life with her family and friends. She added magical moments to our book of memories. She taught us that when Jesus is all we have, Jesus is all we need. She showed us how to embrace life to its fullest and, when it's time, how to say good-bye.

What Do We Tell the Children?

by Cheryl Salem

Nothing is more precious than a child's faith. So many children were praying for Gabrielle: her brothers, her cousins, all her little friends and many in churches across the country who didn't even know her. One little boy came to visit her just a few weeks before her home-going. When he left that day and got in the car, he said to his mama, "Gabrielle's going to be raised up tomorrow."

When she went home to be with the Lord, the cry of my heart was, "Lord, I don't want anyone's faith to be bruised by this, especially not the children's. They have been praying and have put their faith on the line. What do we say to the children? I want them to know the Word still works. You're going to have to give me the words to speak, because I don't know how to help them."

Gabrielle had lots of little friends, and several of their moms came to the house and called the day Gabrielle went home. They didn't know what to tell their children and I made the mistake of saying, "If you can't handle it, just bring the kids here and I'll deal with them."

Hold Fast to the Truth

I had no idea what I was going to say. When the first little girl came, I told the Holy Ghost I couldn't handle it. He graciously came to my rescue and, as soon as I held her in my arms, I said, "Let me tell you one thing. You stand fast and hold on to what is true. Jesus *is* the Healer and He does not lie. He loves Gabrielle, and He loves you. He wants you to carry on the work that Gabrielle started. What Satan meant for harm, God will turn around for good and will multiply what Gabrielle began through you." I commissioned each child to whom I talked to be God's ambassador and carry on Gabrielle's work to fulfill her destiny.

Commissioned for the Kingdom

I commission every person who reads this book to carry on Gabrielle's work to advance the kingdom of God on this earth. I charge you parents to put the Word of God into your children and command the Word to work in their lives. I pray that Gabrielle's anointing will be transferred into you and your children so that the work she began can be multiplied to crush the head of Satan under your feet and finish the course.

I shared with you in the chapter 14 what happened when Harry woke me up and told me Gabrielle was gone. I immediately started praying and calling her spirit back. In the process I woke up Roman, our nine-year-old son, and he crawled up on the bed and laid his head on her chest. Over and over he said, "I speak life to you, Gabrielle. You shall live and not die. I speak life to you, Gabrielle."

When it became obvious she was really gone, Roman cried and said, "You told me if I spoke life to her, she wouldn't die."

Focus on Jesus

Harry and I wrapped our arms around him, and we all cried together. Then we explained as best we were able at that moment that it was Jesus who came for her because He loved her so much and that we would all be with her again someday. Roman has so much of the truth of the Word in him that he was able to accept that God has a plan that we don't always understand. Even when his heart was aching for his sister, he kept his focus on Jesus.

A Decision From the Heart

When we received the evil report from the doctors about Gabrielle, Harry and I made a decision that we were not going to tell Gabrielle or the boys that she had a brain tumor or that it was malignant. They knew her eyes wouldn't move back and forth, and whatever was causing it needed to be fixed. We made this choice for three reasons. First, we didn't want to bring in fear, doubt or unbelief from such an evil report. Second, we didn't want to bring questions into their minds that would cloud their focus. Third, it was irrelevant whether it was a stubbed toe, an eye problem or a tumor; we were going to dwell on life, not death.

When it was all over, Harry and I sat down with the boys and explained about the tumor. The boys said, "Why didn't you tell us?"

Harry said, "It wasn't imperative that you knew all that. I'm your daddy, and I made the best decision for all of us— for Gabrielle, for Mommy, for you boys and for me. You just need to trust that I did what I thought was right."

They looked at Harry, and both said, "We trust you, Daddy."

Never Stop Trusting

That response reveals where we were with God as a family. When we found out what we were facing, we trusted God and His Word. We released our faith for Gabrielle's healing and, even to the point of her going home with Jesus, we trusted God. Ultimately Gabrielle trusted God, because she ran from the captivity of her body to the manifestation of her healing.

Ultimately Gabrielle trusted God, because she ran from the captivity of her body to the manifestation of her healing.

Throughout the time of Gabrielle's illness we didn't focus on the problem, we focused on the answer—Jesus! Yes, we faced the problem every single day and did what we had to do each day. However, we kept our focus on the only One who had the solution. The boys saw that and followed our example.

Ask for Supernatural Guidance

The best advice we give to parents who are faced with questions about how much or how little to tell their children about an illness or how to explain death, is to pray and ask the Holy Spirit for guidance. He will give you the right words to speak, just as He did when I took that first little friend of Gabrielle's in my arms. It is imperative that whatever you tell your children is based on the truth of God's Word. That is why it is so critical to deposit the Word into your children and into you on a daily basis—so that when a crisis comes, it is already there to draw upon.

Children at various ages perceive illness and death differently than adults do. You never know what is going on in the mind of a child, and the words you speak to them must be carefully chosen. For example, one mistake people often make is telling a small child that someone who has died is just sleeping. Then the child is afraid to go to sleep at night, because he fears he will not wake up again. We encourage parents to let their children talk about what they are feeling when someone they know dies and ask questions about what they don't understand.

Heaven's Home

The world has a very perverted view of death, and we caution parents to monitor carefully what they allow their children to view and read. We have selected some good biblically based books about heaven to read to our children because we want them to know that heaven is a place of beauty, peace and joy. Death is not to be feared as the world fears it. For believers, it is simply a graduation from life on this earth to a fuller, more joyous life in eternity.

Death is not to be feared as the world fears it. For believers, it is simply a graduation from life on this earth to a fuller, more joyous life in eternity.

Gabrielle's graduation was earlier than we expected or wanted it to be. At six years old, she had accomplished more for God's kingdom than most do in a lifetime. Maybe that is why she went so soon. We are comforted in knowing where she is and that she is completely restored, and when our work on this earth is over we will be with her again.

263

Sweet Sister

by Harry Salem III

Hello, my name is Harry Salem III. This is my letter on my sweet sister, Gabrielle Christian Salem. I am writing this letter not just because of the book that we are writing, but also because I wish to tell the people who cared about Gabrielle how I really felt about her.

Before Gabrielle was born, I begged God for our next child to be a girl. When I found out that we were having a girl, my heart filled with joy. After Gabrielle was born, I was so eager to hold her, and when I did, I felt deep affection for her. Roman and I were mad when we couldn't bring her home from the hospital the first day. During the next couple of years, we became more and more close together.

My favorite memory was when she and I used to play Barbie dolls all the time. When we landed in Los Angeles once, we got a nice van to put all our books and tapes in, but it only had enough room for all three of us to sit in one seat. Gabrielle was two or three at the time. She kept poking Roman and me, and we kept telling her, "Stop. Stop." Dad said, "You two cut it out back there." I said,

"What are we getting in trouble for? She's the one that's doing it."

The second time we went to Los Angeles we did the same thing, but this time she didn't hit us or anything. Mama bought her a pull case to put all of her Barbie dolls and clothes in. She takes it out, sits on my lap, opens it up and tells me, "Let's play Barbie dolls. You be Ken. I'll be Barbie. We'll be married." I said, "If it beats getting me in trouble, I'll do anything." That was my favorite memory.

When I found out that she was very sick, I immediately started to pray for healing and restoration for her. During that time, I started going out and buying presents for her, a lot of which were mainly Barbie dolls. She always watched TV shows, and she saw a big Barbie jet. I asked Daddy if I could go and get it for her. It came with a microphone to make announcements like "This is your captain speaking" and it had stewardesses, refreshments and everything. It made a real jet sound too. She loved it. I got her one of the Tour Guide Barbies, too.

Suddenly one morning I heard loud voices coming from my parents' room. All I heard was Gabrielle's name being screamed over and over. Even though I didn't exactly know what was going on, I immediately started to pray and speak the Word over her. I wasn't sure how long I prayed for her; all I know was I wasn't giving up. When my dad came and told me that Gabrielle had gone home, I started to cry; but after I stopped, I realized something. No matter what my sweet sister went through on earth, she was finally healed; and as a bonus, she was with Jesus. For the rest of the day I comforted people and reminded them of that. So, even though I might not have cried much, I knew that she was finally home, and we will see her again someday.

It was hard at first for me to lose Gabrielle, but then I realized it wasn't losing her that made me feel sad, it was seeing how Mama and Dad felt when they lost her. That really made me upset because Gabrielle was important to me, but she was more important to the people that gave birth to her and raised her to be a proper young lady. And the day she went to heaven, I did cry, but then I stopped because I wanted to help Mom and Dad get through their mourning. I stayed with Daddy, and we talked and held each other, and we got through it. Mama was the one that took it the hardest. I sat with her with my Bible, and we all just sang hymns, and I was praying and asking God to comfort everyone.

I do miss Gabrielle, but I believe that I should be strong and a comfort when I think of her and miss her, because in heaven she is more alive today than she will ever be on this earth.

The only regret that I have is not being able to teach her to ride that new bike she got. I asked Dad if I could teach her to ride it when she got well, and he said, "Sure." Now I know Jesus was probably the first One to get to teach her how to ride a bike.

Picture Perfect

by Roman Salem

When Mommy asked me what I wanted to write about Gabrielle for the book, I said, "I can say it all in one word—*perfect*. She was perfect."

I remember when she got her Barbie car; she tried to run me over! She played lots of tricks on everybody. One time she put the microphone from her Barbie jet right next to my ear at six o'clock in the morning when I was sleeping and yelled, "Wake up!" Once we "silly-stringed" both of our aunts. Another time we hid under the covers and squirted them with the Super Soaker. She was really cool for a six-year-old and fun. She had lots of friends. She was good in school and good in games. She was perfect.

She looked like me! (Ever since she was a baby, we always called Gabrielle, "Roman in a dress.") She was nice and pretty. She had so many hair things and Barbies that we had to put them out into the hall.

She liked to stick with her family. I wouldn't spend the night at my aunt's house because she wanted me with her. I felt better when I was near her. She always said something funny and made me laugh!

She loved to play Barbies. I couldn't do Barbies, but she used my toy guys to be the husbands and limousine drivers. Sometimes she pretended to gag them and everything.

We had a Nintendo 64 game that she always beat us at. She tried to run us off the road. The little Mario would go "Wahoo!" all the time. We played it almost every day.

Pastor Ron Clark in Florida had a daughter named Amanda who was really good friends with Gabrielle. She had a big collection of dolls and everything that they played with. Pastor Clark took us to Disney World, and Gabrielle loved it. When we got home, Pastor asked what she would like when she got to heaven, and she said, "A big Disney World!"

Another pastor friend in Louisiana owns about four four-wheelers that are really cool. Gabrielle rode them and wanted to go faster and faster.

Pastor Tipover (Dave Williams) would come to our house and cheer everybody up. We call him that because about two years ago he tipped us over on the jet ski he and I were riding. Gabrielle was on the other jet ski, and she was falling over laughing.

Another pastor, Eastman Curtis, came over all the time. You can't pay him to stop smiling. Eastman is the funniest. He's cool. He owns a little motor scooter. He's old and he's like ten. Harry says Eastman is like a big brother at heart.

I had a nickname for Gabrielle. It was "Goober." If anybody bothered her, she'd punch 'em!

She taught me that you should be brave and that you should fight. I'm proud of "Goober" because she was brave and exciting even when she was sick. Even with her backpack of medicine, she still sang and prayed for people. She went to every service we did. And that was good! She brought people to the Lord.

I tell people that it's really hard to lose somebody, but you know they are in a better place and you'll seem them again someday. I can't wait to see Gabrielle. It's tough, but they'll make it through. And not to quit 'cause it'll get better. It's hard, but like Dad says, "It takes any old fish to go downstream, but it takes a live one to swim upstream." It's hard, and you have to push until you get through it. And if whoever is sick owns a Super Soaker, don't get mad. Just love them and spend time with them.

Friend Forever

by Sara Baty

I met Gabrielle, my best friend, when I was five and she was four years old. We liked each other from the very beginning. We loved playing with Barbies and doing lots and lots of art projects together!

Gabs and I would laugh and play jokes on each other too. We enjoyed going to a few ORU basketball games with her family. Many times I got to spend the night at her house when she and her family were in Tulsa. We became best friends quickly!

I was very sad when she started getting sick and not feeling well, but it never stopped us from getting together and playing! One time I made my Mom cancel another friend's birthday party, just so I could spend the night with Gabrielle. Even when she was very sick, we still really loved each other's friendship.

Gabs was out of town a lot, and I missed her. I miss her even more now that she is gone. Our friendship will be FOREVER, and Gabrielle will always be my best friend. I think of her every day. She is the brightest shining star!

God Says, "Well Done"

by Harry Salem

Doesn't every child desire and need to hear words of affirmation from his father? Even Jesus needed to hear these words from His Father as he was about to start His ministry on earth:

> *"This is My beloved Son, in whom I am well pleased."*
>
> MATTHEW 3:17 NKJV

As we fought the battle for Gabrielle's life and walked through the valley of the shadow of death with her, we developed such compassion for the caregivers of those who are sick or infirm. We want to say to every one of you, "Be encouraged, and don't give up the fight." We know that the heavenly Father is also looking down on you and saying, "Well done!" Every situation is unique, and we haven't walked in your shoes, but we love you for where you are walking.

For those of you who are caregivers or who may suddenly find yourselves in the position of receiving an evil report from a doctor for a loved one, we want to share with you what we have learned.

(1) Be Prepared Spiritually

No one can ever be totally prepared for such a crisis, but there are some ways in which we can be prepared spiritually. We have said numerous times throughout this book how important it is to get the Word of God firmly planted in your life and the lives of your family members. Make it a daily practice to pray the Word out loud over your family and circumstances. Don't wait until a crisis hits. Make deposits now so there will be something there to withdraw when the need comes.

(2) Dress for Battle Daily

In the eleven months of providing twenty-four-hour-a-day care to Gabrielle, there were times when we became weary and didn't know if we could go on. It was especially stressful for Cheryl, because Gabrielle looked to her for everything. Once Cheryl became her caregiver, she wouldn't let any other medical personnel touch her. Mommy had to do it. Then we had the added stress of trying to travel to continue with our ministry, which created some unusual challenges.

We dressed for battle every day by putting on the full armor of God. Sometimes there was nothing more we could do but just stand, as this Scripture says:

Therefore take up the whole armor of God, that you may be able to withstand in the evil day, and having done all, to stand.

EPHESIANS 6:13 NKJV

Make sure you put on your armor every day, use the weapons God has given to you and stand firmly on the Word, no matter what happens.

(3) Research What Is Available in the Natural Realm

When you receive an evil report, don't just accept it as fact. Seek additional medical opinions and research what treatment options are available. The Internet is a tremendous resource for doing quick and thorough research. Gather as much information as you can *before* making any decisions.

The moment I heard the words "brain tumor" and then the more definitive diagnosis of "glioma," I started researching and talking with other doctors and knowledgeable people about it. I was not going to leave one stone unturned. In our particular case, the doctors gave us no hope and said chemotherapy and radiation were not viable options. We sought another medical consultation with an expert in New York City. Then we heard about the clinic in Houston with the experimental medical treatment.

About that time John Hagee, a pastor in San Antonio, Texas, called and said, "We prayed a little girl named Lizzie through this same diagnosis, and her tumor was even larger than Gabrielle's. The doctors had told her parents she would die, but God miraculously healed her." (Lizzie is now nineteen years old and serving the Lord fervently.)

John's frankness got my attention as to what we were dealing with. I shared with him what our options were with the clinic in Houston.

He said, "Look, medicine and prayer go hand-in-hand. If she were my child, I'd do anything in my power to help her. We will pray." That church fasted and prayed for Gabrielle through the entire year. They never stopped.

Lizzie's daddy called, and we talked on the phone. I told him what was available. He said, "That wasn't available to us at the time."

"What do you think?"

"I would go ahead and do it."

God is the God of all good things, and every good and perfect thing comes from Him. (James 1:17.) If medicine has been created to help you, then you aren't copping out on your faith by taking every good and perfect thing that God has given you. We made the decision to go to the clinic in Houston.

(I want to take a moment to say that after walking where we have walked, I truly admonish the FDA and even at times the medical profession for their lack of humanity and compassion. There are many who are making strides to bring new treatments and methods to the sick and dying, and their efforts are needlessly hindered by a heartless bureaucratic system often driven by greed. Many changes are needed as to how information and care are made available to people who are facing life-and-death situations.)

You will have to search for the options and then pray about what the Lord wants you to do. It is a tough position to be in, but you just have to do the best you can with the information you have to make a decision, and then trust God. He will see you through.

(4) Surround Yourself With People of Faith

Receiving a bad report from a doctor, as we did, is like being kicked in the gut by a mule. It knocks the wind right out of you. The best advice we can give you when this happens is to surround yourself with people of faith to help you regain your focus and get on the right track. Cheryl and I could not have made it without the loving support of so many wonderful family members and friends. They saw us through not only the initial shock of the evil report but all the way through the crisis and beyond.

(5) Beware of the Lies and Deceptions of the Health Care Bureaucracy

Be prepared to battle the bureaucratic health care system. We became quickly disheartened with the medical

275

community in many aspects from the very beginning of Gabrielle's illness. We know there are many wonderful physicians and healthcare professionals, but unfortunately you must be aware of what the rules are and how to fight your way through the system. Cheryl quickly learned how to deal with the doctors and nurses, and I took on the bureaucrats. Many times we had to stand our ground to get what we needed. Here is an example of what I mean.

Having to do three blood draws a week and traveling across country, we probably had contact with over 125 laboratories or hospitals. At one hospital in North Carolina, I took the blood sample in to have it processed, along with Gabrielle's medical records and doctor's orders. A lady from a church where we were ministering had called ahead to have it all set up. However, the woman at the desk had other ideas. She said, "The hospital cannot process the blood without an order from an in-state doctor. It's the law. You are going to have to go through the emergency room."

"I have been in over 100 hospitals in seven states, and it is *not* a state law."

"It's a federal law."

"It is not a federal law. It is a hospital policy that you want me to go check in to the emergency room so you can hit me with a $250 emergency room visit and see the emergency room doctor so he can hit me with another $200 charge."

She ducked her head and mumbled, "You're right."

Two minutes later the phone rang, and it was a doctor who was a member of the church at which we were ministering. He said to the woman, "Do the blood work now. I am authorizing it."

We learned we had to be forceful and not back up. Interestingly enough, by the time we left that community the following Monday, Gabrielle's picture and petition of Scriptures was posted on the wall of that hospital clinic. Someone from the hospital had come to our services and brought the picture back so people could pray for her.

Be prepared to stand your ground and fight for what is needed and what is right for your loved one. Don't back down.

(6) Don't Stifle Emotions or Communication

Holding back emotions in a time of mourning simply delays the restoration process. When Gabrielle graduated to heaven, Cheryl and I were so focused on dealing with our own emotions that we didn't realize we were stifling our boys' emotions. In the beginning I said to the boys, "Don't talk to Mom about Gabrielle. It hurts her too much." We took all of Gabrielle's pictures down and put them away because it hurt too much to look at them. We didn't recognize how hard we were being on the boys. They missed their sister, but they were trying to be strong for Mom and Dad and, therefore, didn't have any outlet to express their own emotions.

277

We noticed that we were lashing out and taking out our frustrations on the boys. Nothing was the same. There was an empty chair at the dinner table. If we bought a three-pack of Kit Kat® bars, there was one left over. So, we would avoid setting the dinner table or buying the Kit Kat.

We didn't think Harry missed her. We thought he was oblivious to it. Actually what he was doing was trying to be the strong one in the family. He determined he was just going to be stalwart. He would come up and put his arm around Cheryl trying to comfort her silently. All of Roman's mannerisms were so much like Gabrielle's, and he would say, "I know Gabrielle isn't here, but is it okay if I think about her?" "I know Gabrielle isn't here, but…."

It was only a matter of time before something had to give. They couldn't hold their feelings inside forever. This time came in late June and early July. We were working on a message titled "What's in the Box?" The idea came from an old Andy Griffith show. An old man from Mayberry ran out of money, and when they opened up his strongbox what they found was whalebone, a spoon with the skyline of Minneapolis on it and a 100-year-old bond that didn't look like it was worth anything. However, those items were special mementos of his life.

I opened up Harry's little strongbox, and there was his wallet, his money, a letter from his grandma and his pictures of Gabrielle. What was in the box was what was in his heart. I opened up Roman's box and it was the same thing—his wallet and pictures of Gabrielle. I sat them down and said, "Okay, guys, what's going on?" Basically they said, "We can't forget our sister."

"Harry, why don't you want to travel?"

"I just want to stay home awhile."

Home was where we were nesting with Gabrielle. Home was where she was. I said, "What is *really* bothering you?"

"Mama gets mad at me. You get mad at me. I can't even talk about Gabrielle."

"I didn't know you wanted to talk about Gabrielle."

"I miss her. I miss her sitting down in her room. I miss going and playing Barbies with her. I miss listening to her sing while I'm sitting in my room. I miss bringing her new Barbies."

"You need to talk about it?"

"Yes."

"It's fine to talk about it. Mama and I can handle it." We talked for about an hour and a half.

Cheryl and I had been stifling their emotions to a dangerous point. So we started talking about Gabrielle. At the breakfast table someone would say, "I wonder what Gabrielle is having for breakfast this morning." When we walked into church one night, Little Harry said, "I wonder what Gabrielle would be doing right now."

"I don't know. What do you think?"

"Well, she'd probably be calling Roman over to the drinking fountain and trying to stick his head in the water. She just loved to pick on Roman."

Roman is always referring to what she is doing *now*. "You know, Dad, she's up there with her Super Soaker playing with Grandpa."

In January we were talking about how she died. The story we really want to tell is how she lived. Harry is saying how she lived. Roman is saying how she is living. They have taken us away from Gabrielle sick in the bed to what she did up to that point and what she is doing now. That is really a key for us. They have helped Cheryl and I take our focus off what Gabrielle went through and focus on the good memories and thoughts of her. That has helped to speed up the restoration process.

Every family member must be allowed to grieve in his or her own way. Harry didn't *appear* to be grieving, but he was missing her deeply and needed to talk about her. Cheryl couldn't bear to look at her pictures, but Little Harry and Roman needed to remember her as the beautiful little sister that she was and is.

Keep the lines of communication open and don't try to hold back your own emotions or anyone else's. Tears are healing to the soul, and good communication is vital.

(7) Seek a Place of Neutral Ground

When it comes to selecting a place for a funeral or memorial service, we strongly recommend selecting a neutral place. We chose to have Gabrielle's home-going celebration service at the T.L. Osborne building instead of our home church. The reason was that we didn't want to sit down and see her casket in our mind's eye every time we went to church afterwards. We chose not to have it at the funeral home because we wanted the service to be in a place where there was a spirit of life, not a spirit of death. Besides, the funeral home wouldn't have been large enough to handle the number of people that would be coming.

(8) Let Go of Guilt and Condemnation

It is time to turn loose of that ghost of guilt that is hanging on your shoulders. You do the best you can do, and that is all you can do. The rest is up to God. Guilt and condemnation don't come from God. They are tactics of the enemy to keep you in captivity. Guilt keeps you in grief.

The enemy often uses people to bring guilt and condemnation upon you. We were actually criticized by people who had seen us on television and heard us say we had released Gabrielle from the covenant we had made with her. They wrote to us and said, "You were the ones who let her die. You've hurt people's faith all over America because so many people were hurt when she died. If you had stood in faith and never released her, she wouldn't have died. You need to tell people *you* let her die."

It is incomprehensible what people will say at such times. Guard your heart from their words and release such people to the Lord for Him to deal with. Remember two things about such people. First, they have never been through anything in their lives like we went through or like you are going through. Second, they are sent to hold you in the captivity of guilt and to heap condemnation on you. We couldn't listen to such people, and you shouldn't either. Listen to God. The only people you should be listening to are those who are trying to get you out from under the blanket of condemnation and away from the captivity of guilt. We threw that letter in the trash.

We felt no guilt or condemnation that we released Gabrielle. I felt a tremendous and awesome responsibility that morning of November 23, but someone had to make the decision. We were just bystanders and observers taking in God's perfect plan. It wasn't our perfect plan; it was God's perfect plan.

At times such as these, you have to stand up and make a decision regardless of what other people think. You need to stand for something, or you will fall for anything. This is a perfect example. When I hear Cheryl's voice, I know it is my wife. When I hear the voice of condemnation, I know it isn't the voice of God or reason. It comes from the pit of hell.

It is easy to look back and try to second-guess what you might have done different. One thing we learned is that there is no room for "what ifs" in the restoration process. It is time to move to the next level and start eating adult portions at the King's table.

Father God is saying to you, "Well done! Well done!"

Adorable Warrior

by Mel and Desiree Ayres

Our lives have been enriched by our cherished friendship with the Salem family. We had been pastoring In His Presence Church for a few years when a young couple at our church recommended Harry and Cheryl to minister at one of our services. I had remembered seeing Cheryl minister at a women's meeting where she got sick and threw up in the middle of her preaching. She asked the pastor's wife for a trash can, wiped her mouth off and continued preaching, as she said, "I'm not going to let the devil keep me from preaching the Word of God!" She became my hero and role model of faith. Mel and I looked forward to having them come to our church.

Their family ministry encouraged my heart to have children after seeing how children easily fit in and belonged with their parents in the ministry. Joshua Christopher Ayres is a part of our lives now, thanks to the ministry of the Salem family.

We knew this was a divine kingdom relationship for us. Not only had we fallen in love with the Salem family, but our entire church had, too. When news hit of the attack on

Gabrielle's life, the church went into battle with us alongside the Salem family. We fasted and prayed for thirty days.

Cheryl was scheduled to do a fashion show for us and had to cancel due to the life-and-death battle with Gabrielle. God led us to continue with the fashion show. Each lady brought and modeled her own outfit from her closet, and we auctioned off the outfits, turning the fashion show into a fund-raiser to help with Gabrielle's medical bills. The church pulled this heart-warming event together in love for the Salem family. It was our way of saying, "We love you. We are praying for you, and we want to help you in your time of need."

Carman, a long-time friend of Harry and Cheryl's, was eager to help, and he became our auctioneer. Believers' Family Fellowship (Pastors Ron and Melody Villar), another of the Salem's divine kingdom relationships, also joined in on this special day dedicated to our precious Gabrielle.

Gabrielle's home-going into heaven has brought a clearer reality to us of how short life here on earth is, how long heaven is and how important it is as believers while here on planet earth to get as many souls into heaven as we can. As we have been inspired to share stories about Gabrielle and her life, many have given their hearts to Jesus. Souls are still coming into the kingdom because of this adorable warrior. Her life was a full-time ministry for the Gospel, for bringing souls into God's kingdom. She most certainly has heard the Father say, "Well done, good and faithful servant!"

We love you dearly, Salem family.

17

"Ya Come to My House!"

by Cheryl Salem

Gabrielle Christian Salem was definitely "Miss Hospitality." She loved having people come to her house. Her favorite people frequently received anonymous phone calls with a special invitation given: "Ya come to my house?" She never identified herself, but everyone knew who it was and accepted the invitation as quickly as possible.

Gabrielle never lost her joy. She was as silly and funny at ninety-seven pounds as she was at thirty-seven, and she loved to play jokes on people. Eastman Curtis arrived at the house one day with a present that brought her hours of delight. It was a Super Soaker water gun, and she would convince one of her brothers, or anyone else who would be her partner in crime, to fill the Super Soaker with water. Then she would call someone on the phone—perhaps Aunt

Lindsay or Uncle Richard—and give her special invitation, "Ya come to my house?" Her partner would then wheel her outside beside the garage, where she would lie in wait for her next victim to arrive. As soon as they stepped out of the car, she would soak them from head to toe, giggling with delight at every squirt. Her friends and family soon learned to bring more than one change of clothes with them if they received one of Gabrielle's invitations. She was especially delighted to soak her Uncle Richard, who never had a hair out of place. She made his hair her target. You have to know Richard Roberts to appreciate the joy he brought to her by allowing her to destroy his perfect hairstyle.

Gabrielle is still giving her invitation, "Ya come to my house?" She wants everyone to come to her new house in heaven.

Everyone loved Gabrielle. During her illness people from all over the world responded with their love for her by sending over 1000 Barbie dolls, beanie babies, coloring books with crayons and colored markers, frilly dress-up clothes and costumes, such as the outfit the princess wore in the movie *Aladdin*. She had such a giving heart that she delighted in giving these away when other children came to the house. We boxed up seventy-seven U-haul boxes of these items. At the appropriate time, some specially selected items will be displayed in her treasure chest at the

Gabrielle Christian Salem Dormitory at ORU. The remainder will be used to bless other children.

Gabrielle is still giving her invitation, "Ya come to my house?" She wants everyone to come to her new house in heaven. She loved giving away WWJD bracelets to everyone she met and everyone who came to her house. She wanted everyone to know her Jesus. Many people know *about* Him but don't really *know* Him as their Lord and Savior, as a Brother and as a Friend. That is how Gabrielle knew Him, and she shared her faith with everyone who would listen— and even with some who didn't want to listen.

Do you want to *know* Him the way Gabrielle does? Do you want to be the kind of militant warrior she is for the King of kings? If you do, then pray this prayer out loud to the Father:

> Father, I know that You beckon me to *choose* life, as it says in Deuteronomy 30:19. I know that life is made up of a myriad of choices. I come to You now and give You my life. I give You 100 percent of me. I *choose* to serve You, God. I give You all of my hopes, my dreams and my desires. I choose to be like You, God. I choose to be pure. I choose to keep my tongue, and I choose to keep my temper. I choose to be happy. I choose to pray.
>
> I thank You, Father God, that You are a good God and that You are looking for militant warriors in the spiritual realm. I want to become the fighter You want me to be so I will defeat the devil on a *daily* basis, not just when I get excited in church. Father, I thank You that because I revere You, You will show me how to always

choose the best! Lord, I will be careful to give You the glory and the praise. In the precious name of Jesus, amen.

Are there loved ones you have been praying for to *know* Him? We have written a powerful mini-book titled *Speak the Word Over Your Family for Salvation* that you may want to read. Here is one of the prayers, based on John 3:16 AMP, from that book into which you can insert the name of a loved one:

> For God so greatly loved and dearly prized the world
> that He [even] gave up His only begotten (unique) Son,
> so that _____, who believes in (trusts in, clings to,
> relies on) Him shall not perish (come to destruction, or
> be lost) but _____ has eternal (everlasting) life.

There are forty days of such prayers in this book. It is the best way to put your faith into action for those you love.

> *Gabrielle's story is not about death. It is about eternal life.*

Gabrielle will be so excited to welcome you and your loved ones to her house in heaven. She may even have her Holy Ghost "Super Soaker" filled with water from the "River of Life."

Gabrielle's story is not about death. It is about eternal life. She was our best seed, and she is planted in heavenly soil for a purpose—to bring eternal life to all who will hear her testimony and humble themselves before the Lord of lords and the King of kings.

Gabrielle Christian Salem's purpose is being fulfilled as her story goes forth around the world via television, through this book and as her family ministers in churches and conferences. Another way Gabrielle is reaching the nations is through the Gabrielle Christian Salem Dormitory for women, which has been established at Oral Roberts University as a memorial to her. The women on campus at ORU are already calling it "Gabrielle's House." In the lobby will be a beautiful portrait and statue of Gabrielle and a glass case displaying her favorite Barbie dolls and toys. This dormitory will house young women who will be trained and sent forth to every nation. We believe they will carry her anointing upon them as they preach the Gospel of Jesus throughout the world.

Precious Soldier

by Pastor Rocky Bezet

The Salem family came to our church to minister in March of 1999 during Gabrielle's fight for life. "Gabs" inspired our whole family as we witnessed her tremendous courage in the face of such a battle.

Gabrielle played with our daughter—running, jumping on our trampoline and acting as if everything was fine, all the while carrying a fifteen-pound backpack with her treatments everywhere she went.

She was scheduled for an MRI while she was here with us. Members of the Salem and Roberts' families flew in from Tulsa and marched and prayed, wearing "Wahoo! God is Able" buttons and proclaiming faith and trust in our God as the four-hour procedure was being done that afternoon. When the time came for the service that evening, Gabrielle opened the service by singing the glory of heaven into the sanctuary while still wearing that backpack! Not only was Gabrielle one of the most beautiful children anyone ever laid eyes on, but she also had a powerful anointing to minister, as only she could do.

The Salem family stood in unity to bring the Gospel to our hearts, as Little Harry and Roman also sang. Harry and Cheryl then preached a message titled "Restore!" with such conviction and anointing that every heart was changed. We witnessed a true testimony of courage and trust that all began with one little girl's inspiration to stand and minister when most anyone else would have stayed home in bed!

My family was not only blessed to have known such a precious soldier of God's army, but our lives were changed forever. We will never be the same. The memories we have of Gabrielle will be with us always, to encourage us throughout our lives until we see her again.

I know she is singing and praising the Lord Jesus, and I can only imagine heaven rejoicing as Jesus took her to her new house! We love you, Gabs, and we cherish the time we spent with you.

Restoration Is in the House

by Harry Salem

What has been stolen from you in your lifetime? Was it a family member or loved one, finances, a home, a business or career, a dream, your health, your marriage or your joy? Satan is nothing but a bully. If you sit there and take what he is dishing out, he will steal everything you have—your family, your money and your future. Whatever he has stolen, I'm here to tell you that *today* is the day to draw a line in the sand and say, "Devil, no more will you steal from me. I'm taking back the ground you have stolen." *Today* is the day to shout, "Restore!"

Restoration begins with a release. When we released Gabrielle, God showed up, and she got her restoration. When we prayed for Gabrielle, we didn't just say, "God, get rid of Gabrielle's brain tumor." That wasn't enough. We wanted her body totally restored to a state better than it had been before she was sick. God did it!

Whatever you have in your hand, release it to God; and get ready for a miracle. Stop looking at reality. Don't look at that empty wallet anymore. Don't look at the sickness. Stop thinking earthly and set your mind on eternal rewards. It is *the truth* that will set you free, not reality. God is trying to tell you that you are a mighty man or woman of courage, and victory is in your mouth.

No matter where you are walking or how much pain you are in, God will take you from mourning to morning as you focus on the answer—Jesus.

Will you shout, "Restore"? Will you be the voice in the wilderness? We have determined in our hearts and minds that Salem Family Ministries is going to be the voice shouting "Restore" across America and in every nation to which the Lord sends us. Will you join us?

Are you ready for your restoration? Are you looking at the truth? Have you released reality? Now shout, "Restore! Restore! Restore!" Keep shouting until you feel the anointing bring restoration. Don't stop shouting. It's up to you. It is time to sit at the King's table. Don't accept child's portions any longer. You're a King's kid. The Lord is opening up a big, billboard-sized window and pouring out His blessings upon you. There is restoration in His house, and He is bringing it to your house as you shout, "Restore!" into your home, your marriage, your children, your body, your finances or whatever it is you need. Be a prophet of your own future as you shout, "Restore! Restore!"

Cheryl, the boys and I join you and shout, "Restore!" No matter where you are walking or how much pain you are in, God will take you from mourning to morning as you focus on *the answer*—Jesus. Now is your appointed time to shout, "Restore!" And I guarantee the Son *will* shine in the morning!

Let the words of one of Gabrielle's favorite songs ring in your spirit as you "Shout!"

SHOUT!

Shout, for the Lord has given us the city.
Shout for the Lord and take no pity.
Shout, for the Lord has given us the city.
Praise the Name of the Lord.

With the high praise of God in our mouth,
And a two-edged sword in our hand,
We're gonna drive the enemy out,
And conquer the promised land![1]

I remember this line from a movie that a boy said after his father died: "It's not how they died that you should remember; it's how they lived." There is a day you are born and a day you die. In between those two days, there is a dash mark as it appears on a headstone, 1993—1999. That dash mark represents everything you do in your life. It is very important, because it determines how people will remember what you did and who you were.

What do you want that dash mark to represent in your life? Will it be for career successes, for houses, cars, boats and all the earthly goods you accumulate—or will it be for the love and compassion you showed to others, for the way you served the Lord and for the souls you won to Jesus?

People are going to remember this about Gabrielle—her smile, the song in her heart, the life she dedicated to serving her Jesus and her invitation, "Ya come to my house?" Her dash mark may have only represented six short years, but it means eternal life to thousands of

People are going to remember this about Gabrielle—her smile, the song in her heart, the life she dedicated to serving her Jesus and her invitation, "Ya come to my house?"

lives that were and still are being touched by a little girl who wanted everyone to know her Jesus and who wasn't afraid to share His love with the multitudes. She will be remembered for how she lived, not for how she died.

We pray this prayer for you and your family:

Lord we pray for every need, every pain in the body, every torment in the mind, for lost loved ones or anything that is needed. You are able, God. Not 30, not 60, not 100 but 1000 times more is what we ask. That's what Gabrielle would ask, because she would only send the best. Lord, we ask that you restore 1000 for one little girl. We claim restoration for families, marriages, children, finances and every need. We can't wrap our arms around Gabrielle, but God, move on each person to wrap his or her arms around loved ones, speak His Word over them and move toward restoration for each family. We commission each one in the name of Jesus Christ of Nazareth. Amen.

Conclusion:

After Restoration Comes Divine Visitation!

Restoration is not the end; it is a new beginning. No matter what sorrow, grief or storm we walk through, we are not without hope, because we have God's promise of restoration. When God restores His people, they don't return to where they were before the storm. He takes them to a higher level and multiplies their blessings to a greater proportion than they ever had in the past, just as He did for Job. Restoration is a process that has a beginning and an end. So, what comes after restoration? How do we move beyond it? What do we *do* with what we have learned and with God's blessings? What comes next?

About nine months into our restoration process at a service in San Diego, California, with Pastor Jerry Bernard, we received this life-changing revelation that answers these questions: *After restoration comes divine visitation!* We immediately embraced that revelation for our family as

Pastor Barnard preached this message from the book of Joel. He spoke of restoration as recorded here:

And the [threshing] floors shall be full of grain and the vats shall overflow with juice [of the grape] and oil. And I will restore or replace for you the years that the locust has eaten— the hopping locust, the stripping locust, and the crawling locust, My great army which I sent among you. And you shall eat in plenty and be satisfied and praise the name of the Lord, your God, Who has dealt wondrously with you. And My people shall never be put to shame. And you shall know, understand, and realize that I am in the midst of Israel and that I the Lord am your God and there is none else. My people shall never be put to shame.

JOEL 2:24-27 AMP

Then Pastor Barnard explained the key that tells us that something comes after restoration. God begins the next verse of Scripture with "and *afterward*." If He says it, He means it. Let's read what comes "after" in these verses:

And afterward I will pour out My Spirit upon all flesh; and your sons and your daughters shall prophesy, your old men shall dream dreams, your young men shall see visions. Even upon the menservants and upon the maidservants in those days will I pour out My Spirit. And I will show signs and wonders in the heavens, and on the earth, blood and fire and columns of smoke. The sun shall be turned to darkness and the moon to blood before the great and terrible day of the Lord comes. And whoever shall call on the name of the Lord shall be delivered and saved, for in Mount Zion and in Jerusalem there shall be

297

those who escape, as the Lord has said, and among the remnant [of survivors] shall be those whom the Lord calls.

JOEL 2:28-32 AMP

God Calls Survivors

Are you going to be a survivor, a remnant? This is very significant because if you don't choose to be a survivor, then this Scripture doesn't mean anything for you. God isn't going to call anyone who hasn't first decided to be a survivor, to be in the remnant. A survivor is someone who is willing to get in the middle of the battle and endure the blood, sweat and tears. Survivors refuse to quit or back down from what they believe. They are the ones who say, "I don't care how it feels. I'm going on with God. I don't care if everyone thinks I'm crazy. I don't care if everybody thinks we have lost the race. We haven't lost the race, because we haven't stopped running. I will not quit."

A survivor is someone who is willing to get in the middle of the battle and endure the blood, sweat and tears.

Too many people quit and give up right at the brink of their miracles. Don't quit. Don't stop. If we can keep going, you can too. If we can keep treading through the blood, sweat and tears, you can too. God isn't finished with you yet. He isn't giving up on you, so don't give up on Him.

Hold on to the promise of restoration *and* to the hope of what comes after restoration—divine visitation.

The Lord walks among us, depositing into each one who cries out to Him his needs. We read that in the above Scripture. He can't deliver you and save you from your troubles and meet your needs unless you first ask Him to do it. Don't let pride, shame or fear stand in your way. The Lord wants to do a work in you, but he needs your obedience and permission.

Hold on to the promise of restoration and to the hope of what comes after restoration—divine visitation.

Prepared for the Visitation

After restoration comes something supernatural from God—divine visitation. What you have walked out, walked through and learned along the way has prepared you for this visitation. Sometimes it is revealed in a dream or a vision. Sometimes the Lord comes in person (Oral has seen the Lord in person, for example). Sometimes it comes through revelation in His Word or through the soft, quiet voice of the Holy Spirit speaking to your spirit. However it comes, God wants to bring you a dream or expand your vision. A dream is born in your heart, but a vision is born in your spirit. Your vision is your purpose.

My dad told me when I was a little boy, "Son, if you do one thing, do it good. *Then* you can do all the things you dream about. If you shotgun it and try to do all the things you want to do at once, you will never accomplish anything. Pick one thing that you do well."

Our family ministry is what we do well. Our vision has been expanded to help other people discover and expand their visions. We do that by sharing our vision.

God cannot use you while you're crying, "I can't do anything. I'm so depressed. I'm so lonely." You are of no value to anyone else in that state of mind. But when you get through that, He says, "*Now* you've been through something. *Now* I can use you."

Just short of a year after Gabrielle's home-going, we received a call that a thirty-nine-year-old minister friend was killed in an automobile accident. The caller said, "Please come and be with us at the home-going celebration. You've got something to say to these people."

Yes, we do. When a tragedy like this hits, it hurts. To be downright honest, it stinks. But you have a choice to make. You can let it tear you down, or you can pick it up and use it to go toward your vision. After the storm and the mourning, the Son comes in the morning bringing restoration and finally divine visitation.

Each step in the mourning and restoration process is a season. Each one passes. With divine visitation comes a release to move up to a higher level and to go beyond the past seasons. We will never forget who Gabrielle is. She will be intertwined in our ministry for life, but we are coming to the end of the intensity of the pain; and when we get to the end of that, He's going to take us further than we have ever been.

His Timing Is Perfect

You can get ahead of your vision, or you can let your vision die on the vine. If you stay in the time frame God has, provision is in the vision. It just comes naturally. No one could rush us through the mourning and grief but, on the other hand, we could not stay in grief. Jesus is the Restorer and the Redeemer. He knows when it is time for your vision to be born.

It's like having a baby. If you give birth to the vision prematurely, it may be aborted. If you hold it too long, it may die in the womb. When a woman is giving birth to a baby, the doctor says, "Now push. Now hold it." He knows the precise moments for each action. That's the way God is. You may be pushing and He knows, "Now is the time to hold it." The holding is the most difficult part of the whole event.

An Agreement With God

Divine visitation is God's way of implanting His vision in your spirit man. The word for vision in the Hebrew means "signifies an agreement." When you embrace the vision God has for your life, you are coming into agreement with God regarding your destiny. You are answering His call to advance His kingdom.

It is time to exercise what God has given you and go after the harvest—multitudes in the valley of decision.

Right now people are waiting for you to figure out that God has called you. People's lives are hanging in the balance, waiting for you to get in the war and lead them where they are supposed to go. Every day you run across multitudes in the valley of decision. These are the same multitudes Joel wrote of after Israel was restored and brought back from captivity. Read what he said:

> *Put in the sickle, for the [vintage] harvest is ripe; come, get down and tread the grapes, for the winepress is full; the vats overflow, for the wickedness [of the peoples] is great. Multitudes, multitudes in the valley of decision! For the day of the Lord is near in the valley of decision.*
>
> JOEL 3:13,14 AMP

What are you doing about it? Are you making a difference, or are you just walking on by? That is your responsibility and my responsibility. We have been fed and fed and gotten fatter and fatter in the spiritual realm. We are just blobs of Word rolling around in the Spirit. It is time to exercise what God has given you and go after the harvest—multitudes in the valley of decision.

Priorities Change

When Gabrielle went home, our vision got wider, bigger. All of a sudden things that were important before weren't important anymore. Some things had begun to grow cold in us while we were in the initial stages of mourning, but as restoration continued hot coals began to heat them up again. All of a sudden nothing was important except bringing people to Jesus. At Gabrielle's home-going we stood up and prayed for the people, imparted the anointing into the people and made a declaration into the heavenlies as we said, "Devil, you will be sorry you started this. We will pull souls that you just knew would never come into God's kingdom. We will pray for them, we will stand for them, we will speak the Word over them until they come in, and you will be sorry you started this." We do this because Gabrielle was the *best* seed we had. We planted her in the *best* soil, in heaven, and it must produce the *best* harvest.

Provision Is in the Vision

You need to start walking in your blessings. Blessings are contingent upon obedience to God's Word. First you have to get the vision. As you are obedient to God in giving birth to the vision, the provision is simply there for you. You never get the provision first. Provision is *in* the vision.

A wonderful example of this is Peter getting out of the boat and walking on the water to Jesus. In the wee hours of the morning Jesus came walking across the water toward the boat full of disciples. You can read about this in Matthew 14, but we are going to paraphrase it for this illustration.

The disciples were afraid and thought they were seeing a ghost. Jesus called out to assure them, saying, "Don't be afraid. It's Me."

Peter said, "If it's really You, bid me to come to You."

"All right. Get out of the boat. Here I am. Come to Me."

So Peter put first one leg and then the other over the side of the boat and started walking toward Jesus. He got all the way to within arm's length of Him when he began to sink. We know that is true because the minute he started to sink he cried out, and Jesus reached out and grabbed him. If he hadn't been within arm's length, Jesus couldn't have reached him.

Provision is in the vision.

Don't Get Distracted

Don't be so sure of yourself when you are close to Jesus that you sink. Don't think that if you're that close you won't be distracted. You see, Peter was walking on that water and the wind was blowing. The spray of the water was hitting him in the face and getting on his clothes and lapping up around his legs. Do you know what happens when clothes get wet? They get heavy. Every step Peter took toward Jesus got harder as his clothes (burdens) became heavier. Everybody thinks that Peter's great vision or his destiny was to walk on water, but Peter's destiny was the same as yours and mine. Peter's destiny was to come to Jesus.

That was his destiny. On the way to his destiny he got to walk on the water. Wasn't that exciting? On the way to her destiny, Cheryl got to be Miss America. She was also crippled in a car wreck, sexually abused for ten years and thrown through three windshields. All these events have taken her to where she was going—to Jesus.

Don't be so sure of yourself when you are close to Jesus that you sink.

Go to Jesus!

People are so afraid they are going to miss what God wants them to do in life. Do any of these questions sound familiar? "Should I do this, or should I do this? I'm not sure what my call is." "Should I go to this college?" "Should I marry this person?" Here is what happens. Whether it is healing, financial blessing or human relationships, each one is between you and Jesus. All these things are between you and your destiny. What we are saying is this: Don't go after the healing, financial blessings or human relationships. Go after Jesus, and along the way you will trip over abundant healing, prosperity, relationships and peace. God is not going to withhold the blessings from you, such as a healing or your children coming into the kingdom. He wants all those things for you. They are between you and your destiny—Jesus. Don't worry if your clothes get heavy or if the cares of life begin to weigh you down, because it doesn't matter *how* you get to Jesus.

Some Christians seem to tiptoe through the tulips. In other words, nothing bad ever seems to happen to them. That is their destiny. Then there are others who get hit and beat and banged until they are down on their knees and then on their bellies doing the military shuffle crawling to Jesus. But they get to their destiny one way or another. Once you've reached your destiny it doesn't matter if you tiptoed through the tulips, if you ran

Go after Jesus, and along the way you will trip over abundant healing, prosperity, relationships and peace.

like a racehorse or crawled on your stomach. What matters is that you got there. When you stand in front of your Savior, even if you're all scarred up, He's going to say, "Well done. You didn't quit. It might have been harder for you than anyone else, but you didn't give up."

We stood in the midst of the fire and were not burned. Our faith is stronger than ever. Satan may try every way he can to kill, steal and destroy; *but* greater is He who is in us than he that is in the world. (1 John 4:4.) We are survivors and more than conquerors through Christ, who strengthens us! Our vision is clearly focused on the multitudes in the valley of decision to snatch them out of the kingdom of darkness and bring them into God's kingdom. Gabrielle is up in heaven cheering us on and waiting for the day she can welcome every one of us to her house. What a party that will be!

Watchmen on the Wall

by Joe & Margie Knight

Helping Harry and Cheryl write this book has been an honor and a privilege, but most of all it has been divine inspiration. As the words flowed onto each page, it was as if each word came from His heart to theirs and then into mine. It has been a work of love. In the process tears have been shed, but more often smiles and even occasional laughter surfaced as the goodness of God's grace and the joy of watching restoration transform this precious family unfolded.

The role Joe and I played in the drama of 1999 during the battle for Gabrielle's healing was that of watchmen on the wall. We weren't able to be with them physically, but we were with them in the Spirit through intercession and prayer every step of the way.

For us the drama began on New Year's Eve, 1998. Joe called me from work that day and, with a sense of urgency in his voice, said, "Something is happening with Harry and Cheryl. Call and find out how we need to pray."

Joe has the heart of an intercessor and hears from the Lord, so I knew something important was in the wind. I wasn't sure if Harry and Cheryl were in Tulsa or traveling, but I called their home and left a message on their answering machine sharing Joe's discernment and telling them we were praying for them.

Never could we have imagined just how serious this urgency to pray was, until two weeks later when we heard the news of the evil report received from the doctors. It was incomprehensible, but we knew how strong this family's faith was and never doubted God's healing, redemptive power. Early on in the ensuing battle the Lord gave Joe another word for Harry and Cheryl not to let this distract them from God's purpose and destiny. They never did.

Having worked on two previous books with Harry and Cheryl, I knew God had an important work unfolding in the midst of these difficult circumstances and urged Cheryl to keep a journal as best she was able. We talked from time to time as the year progressed, and I was always in awe when I hung up the phone how strong and unbending was their faith.

Our hearts cried out when we received the news of Gabrielle's home-going. It wasn't what we expected, but we know without a doubt that God's glory shines forth in triumph. We are so proud of Harry and Cheryl and of Little Harry and Roman. They have walked where none of us ever want to walk and have unselfishly shared their pain and their victory over death so that others may live. This book is a testimony of their unfailing love for Gabrielle but more importantly of their unwavering faith and trust in their Lord Jesus Christ. They are an inspiration to us all.

Gabrielle Christian Salem

Child of *Courage*...Gift of *Boldness*
Child of *God*...Gift of *Eternal Life*
Child of *Hope*...Gift of *Faith*
Child of *Joy*...Gift of *Strength*
Child of *Laughter*...Gift of *Giggles*
Child of *Love*...Gift of *Affection*
Child of *Light*...Gift of Sparkling *Sunshine*
Child of *Miracles*...Gift of *Healing*
Child of *Opportunity*...Gift of *Inquisitiveness*
Child of *Peace*...Gift of *Harmony*
Child of *Praise*...Gift of *Song*
Child of *Promise*...Gift of *Encouragement*
Child of *Prophecy*...Gift of *Proclamation*
Child of *Vision*...Gift of *Discernment*
Child of *Wisdom*...Gift of *Understanding*
Child of *War*...Gift of *Victory*
Gabrielle...Gift from God never to be forgotten!

—Margie Knight
November 24, 1999

Gabrielle Christian Salem

May 26, 1993 . . .

Gabrielle ministering

Gabrielle singing

An Invitation

Gabrielle's entire life was one of invitation. An invitation to experience life and life more abundantly, to feel joy beyond your troubles and problems, right down to her daily invitation to all who ever met her, "Ya come to my house!" She always wanted everyone to come to her house to play and be together.

I believe with all my heart that there's the biggest, pinkest Barbie house on the streets of gold, with a beautiful little lady on the front steps shouting joyously at everyone on the earth, "Ya come to my house!" Are you going to go to Gabrielle's house? More importantly, Jesus is saying, as He said in John 14:1, "Let not your heart be troubled. In my father's house are many mansions. If it were not so, I would not have told you so. I will come again and receive you unto Myself, that where I am, you may be also."

Jesus is calling to your heart today, "Are you coming to My house?"

If you aren't sure where you will spend eternity but you want to be sure, just pray this prayer out loud.

Dear Lord, I want to spend eternity in heaven. I want to spend it with You, Jesus. Please forgive all of my sins and cleanse me from all unrighteousness. I give you my life, all of it. I receive You, Jesus, as my Lord and my Savior. Thank You for making me new through your blood, Jesus. I'm coming to Your house forever. In Jesus' name.

If you prayed this prayer, then you can know that you belong to Jesus and He belongs to you. If you would like someone to pray with you, or if you would like to tell someone, you can call us 918-298-0770 or write us at

P.O. Box 701287, Tulsa, Oklahoma 74170, or reach us at www.salemfamilyministries.org.

If you are born again but you have had loved ones who have gone to heaven ahead of you, we want you to know that Jesus is saying to you, "Well, done." Don't let guilt hold you in bondage. It's over and behind you. Go on to the future. Don't get hung up in the past. God said to us several months after Gabrielle had gone, "Gabrielle is not in your past; she is in your future." Your loved ones who have gone ahead of you are in your future. They are not in your past. Don't look back; run forward to the future. They are waiting for us there with Jesus.

If you are still struggling with letting go, please pray this prayer out loud.

Lord, help me go forward. I don't want to get stuck here. I trust You, Lord, that every good thing You have for me is in my future, including my loved ones. Help me, Lord, to focus on where I am going and not from where I've come. I believe that what I focus on will develop; therefore, Lord, I choose to focus on You, and You will develop in my life. Thank You for taking me through this trial. I choose not to stop here. I walk forward in You, Jesus. I thank You, Lord, and I love You.

When you pray this, believe it. You may have to go back and pray this for several days. That's all right. Just do it over and over until you know it's true.

If you would like to share what God is doing through this book, we would love to hear from you. Whether you need to share your testimony or ask us to pray, we would love to hear from you.

In Christ's healing and victory,

Harry and Cheryl Salem

Endnotes

Chapter 3
[1] Elgin.

Chapter 7
[1] Hall.

Chapter 9
[1] Compassionate Friends.
[2] Ibid.
[3] Salem, p.54.
[4] Ibid., p.56.
[5] Ford.

A Glimpse of Heaven
[1] Springer, cover.
[2] Ibid., p.31.
[3] Ibid., pp.7-8.
[4] Ibid., pp.9-10.
[5] Ibid., pp.32-34
[6] Ibid., pp.41-42.

Chapter 14
[1] Springer, pp.8-9.
[2] Bolton.

Chapter 18
[1] Star.

References

Bolton, Tony and Kim. "Bless You." Servant Heart Publishing, ASCAP.

Compassionate Friends, Inc. Survey of Bereaved Parents: "When a Child Dies." June, 1999. *www.compassionatefriends.org/survey_when_a_child_dies.htm*.

Elgin, Johnny. "Old Enough To Praise the Lord." Second Base Music/BMI, 1990.

Ford, Steven. "This Test Is Your Storm." SyRue Publishing Company/EMI.

Hall, Dudley. Sojourn Church Sermon Tape, Carrollton, TX. September 10, 2000.

Salem, Harry and Cheryl. *An Angel's Touch*. Tulsa, OK: Harrison House, 1997.

Star, Steven. "Shout." Star Family Singers.

Springer, Rebecca Ruter. *Intra Muros, "My Dream of Heaven."* Forest Grove, OR: Book Searchers.

About the Authors

Harry Salem II grew up in Flint, Michigan. After his father's death in 1968 he relocated his family to Florida. In 1980, he joined the Oral Roberts Ministry and at the age of twenty-six became Vice President of Operations and Crusade Director followed by Director of Television Production. In his work as author, television writer, producer and director, he has won several Angel and Addy Awards and most recently has written the successful book *For Men Only*.

Cheryl Salem grew up in Choctaw County, Mississippi, and overcame many challenges to become Miss America 1980. She is an accomplished author, speaker, musician, recording artist and teacher. She has recorded ten albums and CDs and written numerous bestsellers, including her autobiography, *A Bright Shining Place,* and most recently, *The Mommy Book.* She continues to co-host the popular national daily television program *Make Your Day Count.*

Salem Family Ministries focuses on family and restoration. They stress the unity of family, marriage, personal relationships, financial goals and parenting, as well as leading motivational meetings on overcoming obstacles such as abuse, abandonment, poor self-image and financial difficulty. Together they have written over sixteen books, including *An Angel's Touch* (a top-25 bestseller), *It's Too Soon to Give Up, Being #1 at Being #2* and their most recent releases *Speak the Word Over Your Family for Salvation* and *Speak the Word Over Your Family for Healing.* They also have a popular new video and audio series on marriage and family titled *Harvest Time for Your Family.*

When not at home in Tulsa, Oklahoma, the Salems continue to minister full-time throughout the world. Harry and Cheryl have three children, Harry III, Roman Lee, and Gabrielle Christian.

"As always, Gabrielle, our true General in the Lord."

To contact Harry and Cheryl Salem
write:

Salem Family Ministries
P.O. Box 701287
Tulsa, OK 74170

Or visit their website:
www.salemfamilyministries.org

*Please include your prayer requests
and comments when you write.*

Other Books by Harry and Cheryl Salem

A Bright Shining Place
Abuse: Bruised but Not Broken
A Royal Child
The Mommy Book
You Are Somebody
A Fight in the Heavenlies
Warriors of the Word
It's Too Soon To Give Up!
Being #1 at Being #2
An Angel's Touch
For Men Only
Speaking the Word Over Your Family for Salvation
Speaking the Word Over Your Family for Healing

Additional copies of this book and other book titles
from **Harrison House** are
available at your local bookstore.

Harrison House
P. O. Box 35035
Tulsa, Oklahoma 74153

For a complete list of our titles,
visit us at our website:

www.harrisonhouse.com

The Harrison House Vision

Proclaiming the truth and the power
Of the Gospel of Jesus Christ
With excellence;

Challenging Christians to
Live victoriously,
Grow spiritually,
Know God intimately.